COURAGEOUS FAITH

MY STORY FROM A LIFE OF OBEDIENCE

CHARLES F. STANLEY

HOWARD BOOKS
An Imprint of Simon & Schuster, Inc.

New York   Nashville   London   Toronto   Sydney   New Delhi

Howard Books
An Imprint of Simon & Schuster, Inc.
1230 Avenue of the Americas
New York, NY 10020

First Howard Books hardcover edition September 2016

HOWARD and colophon are trademarks of Simon & Schuster, Inc.

For information about special discounts for bulk purchases, please contact Simon & Schuster Special Sales at 1-866-506-1949 or business@simonandschuster.com.

The Simon & Schuster Speakers Bureau can bring authors to your live event. For more information or to book an event, contact the Simon & Schuster Speakers Bureau at 1-866-248-3049 or visit our website at www.simonspeakers.com.

Manufactured in the United States of America

10   9   8   7   6   5   4   3   2   1

Library of Congress Cataloging-in-Publication Data
Names: Stanley, Charles F., author
Title: Courageous faith : my story from a life of obedience / Charles F. Stanley.
Description: Nashville, TN : Howard Books, 2016. | Includes bibliographical
   references and index.
Identifiers: LCCN 2016023411 | ISBN 9781501132698 (hardcover : alk. paper)
Subjects: LCSH: Stanley, Charles F. |
   Baptists—Clergy—Georgia—Atlanta—Biography.
     Classification: LCC BX6495.S753 A3 2016 | DDC 286/.1092
   [B]—dc23 LC record available at https://lccn.loc.gov/2016023411

ISBN 978-1-5011-3269-8
ISBN 978-1-5011-3270-4 (ebook)

To my two devoted staffs at First Baptist Church of
Atlanta and In Touch Ministries,
with my gratefulness for your faithful service.
It is a pleasure and privilege to serve God with you.

CONTENTS

*"The eyes of the Lord move to and fro throughout the earth
that He may strongly support
those whose heart is completely His."*

—2 CHRONICLES 16:9

Foreword

If my sister and I heard it once, we heard it a thousand times, "Andy, Becky, God has a plan for your life and you don't want to miss it." As children, we believed him. Growing up, we watched him. As adults, we are so grateful for him. Specifically, we're grateful he connected the days of our lives with the purposes of God for our lives.

Through the years, we've had a ringside seat for all God's done in and through our dad. He took a poor, skinny kid from Dry Fork, Virginia, and used him to broadcast the gospel all over the world. Long before there was an Internet, my dad's messages were broadcast to every country in the world every day of the week!

While Dad has produced lots of books, this one is special. Though not an official biography, this book chronicles my dad's biggest life lessons within the context of the story of his life. And what a story it is. It's all here. Triumph, tragedy, love, marriage, divorce, poverty, prosperity, opportunity—all lived out under the canopy of God's promises and faithfulness.

Dad never ran from trouble or the trials of life, and that made an incredible impact on my sister and me. In my personal life and ministry, my takeaway from having Dr. Charles Stanley as my father was that everyone can trust God with every outcome. We don't have to manipulate situations. We don't have to be defiant or try and figure out how to always win. Our responsibility is to trust God and leave all the consequences to Him. When we reach a fork in the road or a defining moment of life, we don't need to choose the easiest or most profitable way forward.

My guess is Dad's preaching has already impacted you. Our prayer is that his story of God's faithfulness will impact you as well, that you'll have the courage to face whatever is going on in your life, and that you'll trust God to help you navigate it. After all, as Dad says, "God has a plan for your life, and you don't want to miss it!"

—Andy Stanley
August 2016

1

Beginnings

Amazing grace! How sweet the sound
That saved a wretch like me!
I once was lost, but now am found;
Was blind, but now I see.
—JOHN NEWTON, 1779

"All God's giants have been weak men who did great things
for God because they reckoned on God being with them."
—JAMES HUDSON TAYLOR

Do you believe that God is really good? That is, do you truly have
confidence that the Lord has your best interests at heart? That He has
a purpose for your life and truly cares about you?

We all struggle with these questions at one point or another
throughout our lifetimes because they strike at the heart of what
it means to be alive and enjoy a worthwhile existence full of sig-
nificance, contentment, and meaning.

Through the years, I've found a great deal of comfort and assurance from the stories of men of faith such as Charles Spurgeon,
D. L. Moody, Oswald Chambers, Hudson Taylor, and Leonard

Ravenhill. Time and again, the Father showed each of these men that He is indeed good, that He has a plan for each of us, and that He cares deeply for every one of us as His children. Our lives definitely have a discoverable purpose and can make a difference in the world.

I believe God has shown me these truths as well, and that is why I am following in their footsteps and sharing my story with you. Because the Father has shown Himself to be so loving, so strong, so faithful, and so wise, I cannot be quiet about it—just like the disciples said in Acts 4:20, "We cannot stop speaking about what we have seen and heard." And my prayer is that the following pages will encourage you—not because of who I am, but because of who Jesus is and what He can do in and through your life.

PURPOSED FROM THE START

Of course, you may be thinking, *You don't know where I've come from. I'm not sure God could do anything through someone who came from such a rough start as I did.*

Oh yes, He can. In fact, He even chose the place of your birth for a purpose. Acts 17:26–27 says, "He made from one man every nation of mankind to live on all the face of the earth, having determined their appointed times and the boundaries of their habitation that they would seek God."

In other words, the Father chose when, where, and to whom you and I would be born for His eternal reasons. The location and circumstances in which we began our lives are part of His special plan for us—not to limit where we would end up but as the unique backdrop for the awesome things He can do through a life devoted to Him.

I certainly did not come into the world under the most optimal circumstances. I was born to Charley and Rebecca Stanley on September 25, 1932, in the small farming town of Dry Fork, Virginia, in the same room where my mother had been born. That was just three years after the devastating stock market crash of October 1929 that initiated the Great Depression, the longest and most profound economic downturn in our nation's history. We were grateful that my father had stable employment at the local textile mill.

Unfortunately, just three months after I was born, in January of 1932, my father became deathly ill of a kidney condition called Bright's disease, an illness that would claim his life an agonizing six months later when I was only nine months old. The reality of our situation shook my young mother to the core in a manner that would affect her for the rest of her life. The Sunday before my father passed away, Mother asked him, "What will I do if you die?" She realized we

> *The location and circumstances in which we began our lives are part of His special plan for us.*

would be on our own during a time when a fourth of the nation's labor force was unemployed and in desperate need, and nearly half of the country's banks had failed.[1] How would she provide for us and take care of me, a small infant who couldn't yet fend for himself?

My father had no choice but to reply, "You'll just have to do the best you can." I cannot imagine how it must have broken his heart to say those words to her. But in 1933, during the terrible depths of the Great Depression, they had already been living hand to mouth like so many other Americans. There was no backup plan, no safety net, no insurance, and no hidden store of funds. There weren't any options he could offer her.

So when my father went to be with Jesus, my mother had no choice but to immediately find a job and go to work.

When I think about her courage during that time, it moves me deeply. Caring for a small baby is difficult enough for any first-time parent. And losing the love of your life can devastate even the strongest person. Yet at the young age of twenty-four, my mother, Becca, did both—during an economic crisis that almost crippled the nation and with little help from other family members.

In fact, she didn't even have her mother and father to help her. Her mother, Flora Jane Hardy, had passed away in 1926 when Becca was only seventeen. The school bus had just pulled up and Mother looked out the window and saw her mother drawing water from the well. All of a sudden, Flora let the rope go, grabbed her head, and fell backward—a fatal stroke ending her life instantaneously. My mother got off the bus and never went to school again because she had to take care of her brothers and sisters. Likewise, her father, George Lee Hardy, had gone to be with Jesus in the spring of 1932, just four months before I was born. So she did not even have them to rely upon.

How did Becca survive it all? With prayer and faith in God. My mother always believed that we could trust the Lord for all of our needs.

Did God make a mistake bringing me into the world when it was in such chaos and my father would soon pass away? Of course not. First, through those circumstances, God showed me that we cannot rely on money for our security—we must depend on Him and Him alone. Second, the Lord taught me to look to Him as my heavenly Father and to rely on Him for guidance and provision.

And third, God gave me such a godly example through my mother, who had a tremendous impact on my life. Even before I was born, she dedicated me to the Father for His purposes. She went down behind the house, sat on an old tree stump, and asked God to use me for His glory. That was her heart—fully set on serving Him.

And the way she responded to the adversity she faced—well, watching her deal with all the pressure with such grace affected me profoundly. What were the things she did that influenced my walk with the Lord in such a positive way? They're not as complicated as you might think.

First, my mother taught me to love God's Word. She didn't do this by creating a reading and memorization plan. Rather, she read the Bible to me and explained how important it is to obey the principles that the Father commanded us to live by.

Mother had no formal biblical training and probably didn't even know what the word *theology* meant, but she did the best she could. She demonstrated how to love and apply Scripture by the way she walked with the Lord daily. I remember how we would turn to the index in her well-worn, thick black Bible—which was the only book she owned—and looked up subjects together. Those are times children just don't forget.

When I was a little older, Mother gave me my first study Bible. She wanted me to have exactly what I wanted, so she gave me money and I went to the store to pick it out. I asked the gentleman there what would be a good Bible for me, since I felt called into the ministry. He said if I was going to preach, there was only one Bible I could use—a *Thompson Chain-Reference*. Of course, I knew he had to be right, because that was the exact same Bible my grandfather, George Washington Stanley, had preached from throughout his life. Interestingly, the *Thompson Chain-Reference Bible* was not on display in that store. Like a rare treasure, it was wrapped in brown paper and kept in a secret place under the counter. It cost fifteen dollars—almost two weeks' wages for my mother—but to me it was worth a million.

Second, Mother taught me to pray. She didn't do so by saying, "Go listen to the pastor." Instead, she showed me how to get on my knees before the Father by praying with me beside my bed every night. Why did we have to be on our knees? Because this was the way we showed the Lord our reverence for Him, that we recognized our need to humble ourselves before Him. From early on, Mother showed me the importance of respecting His authority and obeying Him. Sometimes we opened the Bible during our prayer times to receive His direction, which showed me that listening to God is crucial to our walk as believers.

At the time, I didn't realize how much closer this brought us. I would open up to her concerning all the troubles that I wanted her to pray about. Then she would call my name to the Lord regarding those things, building a wonderful hedge of protection around me. I can still remember how she would pray, "Father, please bless Charles and take care of him." Sometimes she would even weep as she prayed, which was difficult for me to hear. I never had a doubt that my mother loved me. Her sweet prayers are etched on my mind, even so many years after she's gone home to heaven. They've stayed with me and have encouraged me through some very difficult times.

Why did we have to be on our knees? Because this was the way we showed the Lord our reverence for Him.

Third, Mother created within me a desire to know God and to depend upon Him for every aspect of life. For years, she worked at the Dan River Mill, which was about sixteen miles from where we lived. I can still recall her showing me her paycheck—she brought home just $9.10 a week and that had to cover all of our needs: food, clothing, rent, and everything else. Of course, the first

thing Mother did was to tithe the little money she brought home—
no matter what. There were many times that I would look at all our
expenses and think, *That just isn't going to be enough*. But she would
say, "We're going to trust God, and He will provide. He has always
been good to us, and He will be faithful no matter what." Repeatedly,
I watched her faith become reality—seeing the Lord supply every
need we had.

So when I got my first job and began earning $4 a week, I never
questioned whether or not to tithe. Mother had vividly demonstrated
that God assumes full responsibility for our needs when we obey Him.

FOURTH, MOTHER TAUGHT ME HOW IMPORTANT IT IS TO OBEY THE
LORD. And her reason was so simple but so profound: *We must obey
God because He is GOD*. She didn't have to give me some big theological explanation. She simply had such a profound respect for the
Father that it impacted me deeply. Likewise, she modeled the consequences of disobedience by how she corrected me. It was always a
proportional response—the degree to which she disciplined me was
always contingent upon how seriously I had defied her.

Mother had two basic strategies for setting me straight. The first
was that she would send me out to get a switch. She never struck me
with her hand because she was wise enough to know it might have
felt like rejection to my young heart. So she always used a switch to
chasten me. But every once in a while, she sensed that I didn't need
a switch; rather, my actions required something much more profoundly life altering: a motherly lecture. I would think to myself, *Oh
God, help me*. By the time she finished, I would be in tears and in full
repentance.

Regardless of which strategy she chose, I always knew my mother
disciplined me because she loved me and wanted the best for me. Of

course, the same is true for God. As Hebrews 12:9–10 reminds us, "We had earthly fathers to discipline us, and we respected them; shall we not much rather be subject to the Father of spirits, and live? For they disciplined us for a short time as seemed best to them, but He disciplines us for our good, so that we may share His holiness."

There are so many ways my mother influenced me that I could go on and on. She taught me to treat others as I would like to be treated and to have a servant's spirit. She exhibited forgiveness, even in circumstances that were terribly unfair. She showed me that when we know the right thing to do, we must complete the task faithfully, be persistent, and never quit. And she always encouraged me to look my best, do my best, and be my best. These weren't lessons she merely told me about—these were principles that she demonstrated with her own life.

ON YOUR OWN?

Of course, you may be thinking, *I didn't have a godly mother like that. My home life was unstable. I was alone.*

Yes, I had a faithful, godly mother, but also one with the burden of supporting us. Sadly, that meant that I was often alone, even as a very small boy, because she had to work in order for us to survive. In fact, she was usually gone by the time I woke up in the morning and couldn't come home until long after my school day was done. Although when she could, my mother arranged for different people to take care of me while she was away, it seemed as if I was by myself more often than not.

In fact, one of my earliest memories is of being only two or three years old, sitting on the bed with a terrible earache. I don't know why that experience made such a profound impression on me, but it obviously affected me deeply because I remember it clearly. I was so miserable and felt so utterly alone because there was no one to take care of me, no one to alleviate the pain, and no one to comfort me. Mother was at work, so I sat alone in our little house with the wooden walls, crying with only a dim kerosene lamp to light the darkness. I remember wondering if my mother had left me forever because her absence that day was so overwhelming and seemed so permanent.

I imagine that part of it was the not knowing when or if I would ever see her again. That's how loneliness works, of course: you begin to think no one will ever understand, accept,

She always encouraged me to look my best, do my best, and be my best.

or care for you again. And in those early years, all we had was each other. If I lost her, I would be losing the most important person in my life. One time, my mother went somewhere on an errand and was gone all day, but she didn't tell me where she was going or when she would be back. I didn't know how to reach her or how long I would be by myself—alone in that quiet, sparse little house. I just kept thinking, *What if she never comes home to me? Who will love me? Who will help me? Why doesn't she stay with me?* It affected me so deeply that I cried until she returned. My fears had been unfounded, of course, but that sense of loss and isolation continued to assault my young heart. Another early memory is of coming home to an empty house after school because Mother worked until about five o'clock. I was in first grade, and like a photograph in my mind, I can still see the long black key that we hid under a brick outside. Only Mother and I knew where it was. But each afternoon as I walked up to the door, I would wonder if the key would be there. What if it was missing? What would I do? After all, it was an extremely important key to my six-year-old mind—the key to where my mother and I lived together, where our belongings were, and where my needs were met. It represented my one place of safety, where I felt my mother's love and care for me. What would become of me if I couldn't get into my home? I always felt relieved when I moved the rock and saw the key was there.

But that relief was only momentary. I would put that big, imposing key in the lock, hear the bolt turn over with a clang, and open the door, thinking all the while, *There's no one here. I'm going to be by myself.* I would dread going inside, not knowing what I would encounter there and loathing the loneliness.

I would try to make the best of it, of course. I became an expert at playing by myself—pretending I was a cowboy by riding a broomstick horse or imagining winning great battles with my hollow-cast metal toy soldiers. As I got older, I collected stamps, built all sorts of model airplanes, and paid close attention to the news, especially world events. I also went to the movies on Saturdays. It cost only nine cents to see a show and five cents for popcorn—and if there happened to be a double feature,

I would open the door, thinking all the while, There's no one here. I'm going to be by myself.

that was a big deal. I could sit there all day, enjoying the adventures of Errol Flynn, Jimmy Stewart, Gary Cooper, Robert Taylor, John Wayne, Roy Rogers, and Bob Hope—along with the newsreels and cartoons they played in between—for only fourteen cents.

But I was still by myself.

And that underlying sense of being alone in the world permeated my life.

That's not to imply I was neglected; it was simply our reality. I knew my mother was doing her very best to provide for me, and I was well aware of the sacrifices she made on my behalf. Even though we were very poor, Mother wanted me to look my best, so every night she washed and ironed my bib overalls for me to wear to school the next morning. I had only two pairs, so they were truly wash-and-wear pants. But she always made sure that my shoes were shined and that I had a handkerchief in my pocket.

During the summer months, Mother would pay Mrs. Cole, a lady with a boardinghouse across the street, to feed me lunch. She wanted to make sure I ate right. Also, if her shift changed and she had to work in the evening, she always left a place set on the table and a meal I could heat up. And I did what I could to help her by washing my dishes when I finished eating.

Mother also did what she could to find people to look after me. For a short time, we lived in a house with Mother's two sisters, Dura and Evelyn, and their husbands. I was very small, but I can remember that big empty house with its long stairwell. Everyone had to work, so they pooled their meager funds and hired a maid named Ada, who took care of everything in the household. This was before I went to school and before I had cousins, so I was home alone with Ada all day long. She cooked for me and took care of my basic needs. Even so, she was not there to have a relationship with me—her focus was to take care of the housework. So more often than not I was admonished to go play by myself and not be underfoot. Still, I thank God for Ada, who took care of me at such a young age.

I also recall that in the first grade, my dear uncle Jack would help me get ready for school—combing my hair and cooking my breakfast. Of course, he had his own job driving a truck for a produce company, so eventually he taught me how to get myself ready for the day and make my own breakfast—usually an egg, a piece of toast, and sometimes even a strip of bacon.

But we moved so many times—seventeen in my first sixteen years—that it was almost impossible to have a sense of stability. North Main Street. Bellevue Street. West Thomas Street. Washington Street. Myrtle Avenue. Campbell Street. Carter Street. Girard Street. With so many different neighbors, friends left behind, and changes in schools, it is no wonder that I felt an underlying sense of loneliness and insecurity.

One Saturday afternoon, my friends Rob and Jimmy came over to visit me. We were having a wonderful time playing games and laughing when one of the boys' fathers came to pick them up in his car. I pleaded with them, "Please don't go," then watched heartbroken as the three of them drove away without me. The sinking feeling of abandonment hit me deep in the pit of my stomach. I clearly remember thinking, *I have absolutely no one.* In that moment, the loneliness weighed on me like a ton of bricks. I felt crushed under the feelings of alienation and rejection, as if there was no one in the world I could count on or rely upon.

It is in recollecting times like this that I realize the ineffective ways I tried to fill my needs for companionship. When I was five years old, my friends and I took an apple off the tree of a neighbor who lived down the street. I knew better than to take something that wasn't mine, of course, but I wanted to play with the other boys. Well, I learned my lesson.

> *I felt crushed under the feelings of alienation and rejection, as if there was no one in the world I could count on or rely upon.*

That neighbor called the police and an officer came and parked his patrol car right outside my house! He stayed there all morning. As you can imagine, there wasn't a kid to be found—everyone went into hiding and disappeared for the rest of the day. I was so scared that

I've never been tempted to take anything without permission since that day.

Another time, I went to the grocery store and charged candy to my mother's account. I threw it up in the air so that my friends would come over and talk to me—I knew they would be excited about getting some candy. I didn't care that I would get in trouble for being wasteful. I just wanted so badly to get them to stay with me longer. That's how intensely I felt the loneliness.

As naïve as my actions might seem now, I can't help but think how adults do the very same things. People rely on wealth, power, beauty, intelligence, or skill to try to attract others and fill their deepest needs.

All of this to say that you may have felt very alone when you were a child, as if there was no one to love or defend you. I had a loving mother, but I certainly understand your loneliness. There were times I felt I had no one. But regardless of whether you were an orphan or had a full and happy family, understand that we all try to find earthly anchors to give stability and meaning to our lives. We crave the visible, tangible reminders that we are worthwhile, loved, respected, and accepted. But any of it can be lost or taken away. And when the world crumbles around us, we realize there is only one Person we can really count on who will never leave us for any reason.

WHO IS WITH YOU?

I wanted to have Jesus in my life at an early age. In fact, I can still remember I was attending a Vacation Bible School at King Street Baptist Church when I was a small boy and I went forward to ask how I could know God. Unfortunately, they just sat me down, gave me a white card to fill out, and then sent me on my way—never telling me how I could have a relationship with the One who sacrificed His life on the cross for me. I knew that wasn't right, so I never went back.

Thankfully, God never gave up on me—just as He doesn't give up on you. Crystal clear in my mind is that life-changing Sunday morning in June 1944 when Jesus finally got a hold of me. I was almost twelve years old, and Mother and I were living on Campbell Street. I took my place at the end of the second row at the Pentecostal Holiness Church of Danville, Virginia. As usual, my Sunday school friends Clyde, James, Tig, and Nelson were right there beside me.

We had a special guest that day—a kind-looking, middle-aged lady named Mrs. Wilson who was preaching revival. Something about the way she delivered that message of salvation struck me to the core. I don't recall everything she said, but I did realize how far I was from the Father because of my sin. She explained that my sin created a chasm between me and the Father, and I could not bridge the gap by my own efforts. But, she said, Jesus had spanned the great divide for me through His death on the cross and resurrection. If I would just ask Him to be my Savior, I would have a real, eternal relationship with my heavenly Father and Creator—the Lord God Almighty.

I knew I did not want to be separated from God for one more minute. When she gave the invitation, I was the first one down the aisle and on my knees. All my Sunday school buddies came up to the altar, knelt down around me in a circle, and prayed, "Dear Lord, please save Charles."

Almost immediately, the heavy weight of my sin and guilt was gone. I had a living, personal, love relationship with God—one "that neither death, nor life, nor angels, nor principalities, nor things present, nor things to come, nor powers, nor height, nor depth, nor any other created thing, will be able to separate" me from (Rom. 8:38–39). It was so profoundly impactful that I was convinced that everyone needed to do the same—I wanted everyone I knew to have the joy and assurance that I'd received.

I especially want you to have it. I do not know how you grew up or what challenges you've had in your life, but there is one thing I understand for certain: God loves you and wants you to experience the wonderful plans He has for your life.

Your heavenly Father sees more in you than you can ever perceive in yourself. From the time you were in your mother's womb, He had full knowledge of your potential (Ps. 139:13–16) and engineered the circumstances of your life so you could know Him and experience the purposes for which you were created (Acts 17:26–27). Encumbered by seemingly insurmountable obstacles or even falling apart, your life may be less than what you expected. Perhaps you have terrible fears about the future or about what you are worth. But the Lord is here for you through it all. He will never leave you or forsake you. And He gives you the wonderful assurance that you are indeed accepted, loved, respected, and worthwhile in His sight. Take it from me, you can overcome anything that happens in your life—regardless of how devastating or hopeless it may seem—by having faith in God. All that is necessary is that you embrace the way He has provided for you to know Him and trust Him to lead you.

Take it from me, you can overcome anything that happens in your life—regardless of how devastating or hopeless it may seem—by having faith in God.

What is the way He has provided? It all starts with accepting Jesus as your Lord and Savior. You see, you and I are separated from God by our sins—the acts we've committed in our lives that are contrary to what He has commanded. I don't need to tell you what your sins are—you know what it is that causes feelings of guilt to rise up within you and makes you doubt your worth. Those sins create a gulf between you and the Lord that is impossible for you to overcome on your own.

This is why we cannot know God without first recognizing what Jesus has done for us. Romans 5:10 tells us, "While we were enemies we were reconciled to God through the death of His Son." Only God's Son, Jesus Christ, could pay the penalty of our sin on the cross, forever spanning that great divide between us and the Lord. It is through His sacrifice that we can have an eternal relationship with the Father that no one can ever take from us.

So how do you take hold of what Jesus has done for you? Romans 10:9 explains, "If you confess with your mouth Jesus as Lord, and believe in your heart that God raised Him from the dead, you will be saved." It is that easy. You say with your mouth what you believe in your heart.

If you've never entered into a personal relationship with God, I encourage you to do so now. Tell Jesus in your own words that you trust Him for salvation. You can also use this simple prayer:

Lord Jesus, I believe that Your death on the cross was enough to forgive all of my sin and restore my relationship with God. I also believe that Your resurrection was undeniable proof that You have triumphed over sin and that You are the only way to have eternal life. I ask You to forgive my sin and be my Savior. Thank You for hearing my prayer and providing the way for me to have a growing relationship with my heavenly Father. Thank You for giving me everlasting life and a home with You in heaven. Help me to walk in a way that is worthy of You and that helps other people to know You as Savior as well. In Jesus' name, Amen.

If you have just received Christ as your Savior, congratulations! You've made the very best decision you could ever make because there is nothing more important in this life or the next than having a personal relationship with God.

As I said, the Father will never abandon or reject you. And if you follow Jesus in faith, certainly you will overcome every obstacle He allows you to experience. You'll discover, as I have, that He is good,

If you follow Jesus in faith, certainly you will overcome every obstacle He allows you to experience.

kind, wise, that He cares deeply for you, and that there is nothing so wonderful as discovering and living out the awesome plan He has for you.

2

Finding Purpose

Take my will, and make it Thine,
It shall be no longer mine.
Take my heart, it is Thine own,
It shall be Thy royal throne.

Take my love, my Lord, I pour
At Thy feet its treasure store.
Take myself, and I will be
Ever, only, all for Thee.
—FRANCES R. HAVERGAL, 1874

"To be much for God, we must be much with God."
—LEONARD RAVENHILL

The truth of the matter is that childhood can be very tough. Whether it is because of a difficult family dynamic, financial problems, physical ailments, early failures, the hurtful things others say of us, or any number of other challenges, the path of our life is often shaped by the events and details that appear overwhelmingly negative during our early years. But if we can find the strength and grace to trust God with those trials and afflictions, He will help us find our purpose as much in the closed doors as in the open ones.

In my early years, I experienced three negative influences that affected my life profoundly as I grew up. But of course, God always counters the effects of adverse circumstances with His absolute truth.

MORE THAN ADEQUATE

The first issue I faced was that from early on I constantly had messages playing in my mind about all the things I couldn't do and could never become. This was for several reasons, of course. The first was that I neither liked school nor did well in it.

I started first grade a couple of weeks before my sixth birthday in September 1938, and I cried every morning that first week. We were seated by last name, so I was always relegated to the back of the class. Of course, that was a valid way to organize the students, but it made me feel as if I were already falling behind somehow.

To make matters worse, I really did fall behind—I didn't make good grades in school in those initial years. Although I worked hard to learn the material, it seemed to be more difficult for me than for the other students. Part of that was because I started school a year before my peers, so I was always the youngest person in my class. Also, from the age of thirteen on, I had a job delivering newspapers. By the time I was fourteen, my responsibilities had grown to a daily route with more than 125 customers. I would get up at five o'clock in the morning, drink a glass of water, deliver newspapers on foot for an hour and a half, come home, eat breakfast, and catch the bus to school. You can imagine how tired I was before my classes ever began, especially when the weather was bad. Then I'd come home after school and repeat my route because back then newspapers put out morning and afternoon editions. Needless to say, I was often exhausted and my grades suffered.

My mother was kind about it, of course. Whenever I brought home a bad report card, she would ask, "Did you do your best?"

I would reply, "Yes, ma'am. It's the best I could do. I'm sorry I haven't done very well."

She would smile at me in such a loving and comforting way and say, "Charles, just do your best. All I ask is that you do your best because then it'll all be okay. God will work it all out." She never discouraged me or berated me for not doing as well as the other students. But it still hurt to know I wasn't measuring up.

I vividly recall how bad I felt in sixth grade. The teacher drew five pictures on the chalkboard at the front of the classroom in order to motivate us. There was an airplane, a train, a ship, an automobile, and a field of sheep. Students who made an A on a test or assignment had their names written under the airplane, indicating that they were soaring high. Students who scored a B were listed under the train, showing they were on the right track. And so it went down the line—C students were under the ship, just sailing by; D's were under the automobile puttering along; and any students who had the misfortune of earning an F were relegated to the the sheep field.

My mother would smile at me and say, "All I ask is that you do your best because then it'll all be okay."

I am certain my teacher had good intentions. I'm sure she simply wanted to inspire us to work hard and reach for our dreams. Sadly, she ultimately achieved just the opposite. Many days my heart sank as I walked into that classroom and saw that "Charles Stanley" was the only name in the sheep field. I felt like it announced to the whole world that I was a miserable failure.

My friends would say, "Hey, Charles, when are you going to get out of the sheep field?" They weren't trying to be unkind, but it bothered me profoundly. I felt incredibly limited and inadequate. Somehow I eventually passed that class, but I don't know how. Maybe the teacher felt sorry for me. And that fear of being inferior persisted.

Thankfully, God used those experiences and feelings of inadequacy to drive me to Himself and to teach me a great deal about serving Him. He showed me how to depend upon Him for everything in my life—not just for His provision, as I spoke about in the first chapter, but also to be fit for whatever He called me to do and to see whatever He allowed me to face as for my ultimate good and His glory.

In fact, a few years ago, I received the sweetest letter from a lady who illustrated this point exactly. She'd heard me tell the story about my struggles in sixth grade and wrote, "Dr. Stanley, When your teacher criticized you for being in the sheep field, she didn't realize that was a word of prophesy that God was going to make you a shepherd!" What a wonderful way to look at it! Certainly, the Father used that experience and the inadequacy I felt to help me be the servant He wanted me to be. I had to be at the bottom so I could faithfully encourage people when they likewise feel low, deficient, and worthless. As 2 Corinthians 1:4 (NLT) reminds us, God "comforts us in all our troubles so that we can comfort others. When they are troubled, we will be able to give them the same comfort God has given us."

If a person who stands up to preach the Word of God supposes he has it all under control, then he has missed the point of what the Father has called him to accomplish and will find himself limited by his own human strength and ability.

Think about it. The word *adequate* means "to be equal to what is required or sufficient for the task." As a preacher, I hope to see eternal change in people's lives that is empowered by the Holy Spirit and glorifies the Lord Jesus. I want to see people break free from their fears and everything that keeps them in bondage. But I must always remember that I am never sufficient to accomplish these goals in the lives of others—this transformation is brought about only by God Himself.

"Dr. Stanley, When your teacher criticized you for being in the sheep field, she didn't realize that was a word of prophesy that God was going to make you a shepherd!"

So ministry is always about the Lord doing His work through us (John 15:4–5). Even the apostle Paul said that we have confidence as believers to achieve whatever the Father calls us to, but that it is "not that we are adequate in ourselves to consider anything as coming from ourselves, but our adequacy is from God, who also made us adequate as servants" (2 Cor. 3:5–6). The Lord is the One who works through us to accomplish all He has planned.

The same is true for you. Did your circumstances early in life make you feel less than enough? The Father may have brought you to a place where you feel totally inadequate and absolutely helpless so that you would place your trust completely and entirely upon Him. Because only then would you trust Him enough to step out in faith in the power of the Holy Spirit.

Why? Because He wants us to live every single day of our lives in complete dependence upon Him—upon His energy, wisdom, and strength. We may imagine ourselves to be ineffective and insignificant, but the Father wants us to rest in His ability and presence so we'll see that "the surpassing greatness of the power" and the victory we experience are because "of God and not from ourselves" (2 Cor. 4:7).

It is the Lord at work in and through you, friend. And He has a wonderful plan for you that is as unique as your fingerprints and designed to give you profound fulfillment and joy. So how do you overcome your insecurity and your feelings of inadequacy?

FIRST, UNDERSTAND HOW YOUR HEAVENLY FATHER SEES YOU. Search Scripture and discover the truth about yourself so when thoughts of inadequacy arise, you can cling to His accurate assessment rather than a faulty view. Ephesians 2:10 declares, "We are His workmanship, created in Christ Jesus for good works, which God prepared beforehand so that we would walk in them." You are specially designed by the Creator for His wonderful, eternal purposes. Regardless of what anyone says, when Jesus is your Savior, you are loved by God and have been accepted into His family forever.

SECOND, ACKNOWLEDGE AND ACCEPT YOUR WEAKNESSES AS AN AVENUE FOR GOD'S GLORY TO SHINE. The famous battle between David and Goliath wouldn't have been special if the two combatants had been the same size and had possessed similar skills. However, because David was a young boy with no armor or experience in battle and Goliath was a nine-foot-tall, bronze-clad seasoned warrior, it was a match to be remembered. No one present would have bet on David for the victory. It was obvious that the Lord's intervention was David's only hope. And so David proudly proclaimed, "You come to me with a sword, a spear, and a javelin, but I come to you in the name of the LORD of hosts, the God of the armies of Israel, whom you have taunted. This day the LORD will deliver you up into my hands, and I will strike you down and remove your head from you . . .

that all the earth may know that there is a God in Israel" (1 Sam. 17:45–46). Thankfully, we know that's exactly what happened. And this illustrates the principle we find in 2 Corinthians 12:9, that God's "power is perfected in weakness." Or as *The Living Bible* puts it, "My power shows up best in weak people." You may feel inadequate in a specific area so that the Father can show His supernatural power through you in that particular aspect of your life.

THIRD, TAKE THE OPPORTUNITY TO ASK THE LORD FOR STRENGTH. Every time you sense those feelings of inferiority creep up, instead of fretting, go to the Father in prayer and acknowledge your dependence on Him. Claim Philippians 4:13 as a promise: "I can do all things through Him who strengthens me." And praise God for assuming the responsibility for all your needs as you obey Him.

FINALLY, STEP OUT IN FAITH. Do exactly as the Father directs you, and allow Him to work through you in ways beyond your imagination. I can promise that you won't be disappointed (Rom. 10:11).

UNCONDITIONALLY ACCEPTED

The second negative influence that shaped my path was that I grew up with some wrong beliefs about my relationship with God. As I explained in the previous chapter, when I was twelve years old, I walked down the aisle and asked Jesus to be my Savior. Right afterward, my pastor called me up to the pulpit and said, "Charles, I want you to tell these people what Jesus has done for you."

I looked out at that big church and said, "I don't know everything He's done, but I know that He saved me."

I will never forget what my pastor said to me in the wake of that life-changing decision. He said, "Charles, you grow up and be a good boy and one of these days you'll die and go to heaven." Unfortunately, he didn't follow that up with, "This is what Jesus did for you at the cross: He gave you His own righteousness so that you would never have to earn your salvation and never have to be afraid of losing it." Likewise, he never said, "Being 'good' will be a lifetime struggle because your human nature and the Spirit of God within you will pull you in different directions. You win that battle step by step by trusting in the Lord." No, he just told me all he knew to tell me: "Be a good boy and one of these days you'll die and go to heaven."

He was a dear man of God who loved the Lord and who certainly loved me. But what he was communicating was that if I wanted to maintain my relationship with the Savior and be accepted by Him, I had to behave a certain way and earn the right to know Him.

It wasn't very long before I realized this was an extremely difficult thing to do—especially because I grew up in a church that had very strict rules. From early on, I was taught that it was wrong for boys and girls to be in the same swimming pool or for women to wear pants or dresses with short sleeves. Likewise, it was considered sinful to go to a movie, even a clean one.

Of course, I've already told you how much I loved going to the cinema on Saturdays. And for the most part, when I was a boy, all the films were very wholesome—especially by today's standards. I can't recall anything I saw back then that ever motivated me to disobey the Lord. On the contrary, many of the films during my early years taught a great deal about character, commitment, sacrifice, and patriotism.

But I remember that when I was fifteen, I went to see a delightful musical called *I Wonder Who's Kissing Her Now*, about the life of songwriter Joseph Howard, who wrote charming old-time tunes such as "Hello, Ma Baby!" and "Goodbye, My Lady Love." I don't know why this particular film stirred such anxiety within me, but I spent the entire time filled with shame, fearing God would destroy the theater with a bolt of lightning. I imagine that all I'd heard in church about the sinfulness of movies was finally taking effect.

All that is to say that my early Christian life was consumed with trying to hold on to my salvation. I read the Bible, prayed, and did whatever I could think of to please God and earn His love—never realizing that Jesus had already done everything necessary to make me acceptable in His sight. Of course, I never felt that anything I did was enough, which it wasn't. I didn't yet understand that Jesus had taken care of the unfathomable penalty for my sin on the cross—a price only He could pay as the sinless Son of the living God. As Ephesians 2:8–9 teaches, "By grace you have been saved through faith; and that not of yourselves, it is the gift of God; not as a result of works, so that no one may boast." His Holy Spirit was not about to let me think I did *anything* to deserve my salvation on my own other than accept Christ's offer. No, His goal was to help me express faith that what Jesus had done was absolutely sufficient, irrevocable, and permanent (John 10:27–28).

The Holy Spirit's goal is to help us express faith that what Jesus has done is absolutely sufficient, irrevocable, and permanent.

So there was always this battle in me between what the Holy Spirit was trying to teach me through the Word and what I thought was true because of what I'd learned in church. In the evenings, I would kneel down by my bed and repent of whatever I could think of. I can remember praying, "Oh God, whatever I've done, please forgive me. Don't let me die without You. Please forgive me, Father." And I went to sleep every night frightened that I was no longer saved. But within me, the Spirit continued to witness to the fact that what Christ had given me was enough and that my salvation was secure.

Thankfully, as I grew up and searched the Word myself, I discovered that many of the things my church said were sinful were not even listed in the Bible. I also realized that believing you can lose your salvation is utterly incompatible with the biblical concept of being saved by grace through faith, as we just read in Ephesians 2:8–9. If we have to do something to keep what Jesus has given us, then that means salvation is by a partnership of faith *and* works, which has no basis in Scripture. Salvation is either by grace alone (which is what we see in God's Word; see Romans 3:23–24; 5:6–21; 11:6), or we achieve it through our efforts (which is the usual path of religion). It cannot be both.

So I went back and looked at all the verses that had formed the foundation of my early beliefs. One by one, I found that I had missed important details in the context of those passages, drawing the wrong conclusions about what they meant.

The pain of fearing daily that I would lose my salvation was overcome when I discovered one of God's most foundational and joyful truths, a principle that could have brought me so much peace and courage as I was growing up. I was sitting in a Greek class at seminary, meticulously translating 1 John 3 from the original language. In the first verse of that book, John talks about the security of our salvation: "See how great a love the Father has bestowed on us, that we would be called children of God; and such we are." Does a father disown his children because they are disobedient? Of course not—at least, not a good and holy Father, such as God is. Earthly fathers may be unreliable about such things, but the Lord is absolutely faithful (2 Tim. 2:13).

Additionally, Romans 8:15 says, "You have not received a spirit of slavery leading to fear again, but you have received a spirit of adoption as sons." Adoption was a very serious matter in ancient times. A parent might be able to renounce a natural child, but by law, one who had been adopted would belong to the family forever. This is why we never have to fear—our relationship with the Father is permanent.

Of course, you may be wondering, *What about when I sin after salvation? Doesn't that separate me from God?* Sin may hinder your fellowship with the Lord, but it will never divide you from Him eternally again. And 1 John 1:9 promises us, "If we confess our sins, He is faithful and righteous to forgive us our sins and to cleanse us from all unrighteousness."

Also, in 1 John 3:2–3, the apostle goes on to explain, "Beloved, now we are children of God, and it has not appeared as yet what we will be."

> *Earthly fathers may be unreliable, but the Lord is absolutely faithful.*

In other words, we're not yet perfect like Jesus is, and we shouldn't expect to be. John continues by saying, "We know that when He appears, we will be like Him, because we will see Him just as He is. And everyone who has this hope fixed on Him"—that is, the expectation of seeing Christ and being like Him—"purifies himself, just as He is pure" (vv. 2–3).

This passage clearly defines our role. After all, children don't train themselves. The Father is the One in charge of His children's education and makes sure they stay on track. So what children must do is watch and obey the Father—trusting Him to (1) provide what they need; (2) keep them safe; and (3) lead them in the right way. Our responsibility is to have our hope and our focus fixed on Christ; His is to purify us. So when we're centered on Jesus, He sanctifies us, instructs us, and empowers us to become everything He created us to be.

This truth takes the pressure off of us and puts the responsibility on God, who is the only One who truly knows how to raise us up as His children. Instead of reading the Bible and praying in order to *impress* Him or to *earn* His favor, we do so out of love and gratitude because we simply want to *know* Him. We look to the Father, learn from Him, and obey as He instructs, knowing He is faithful to redeem and transform us (Rom. 12:1–2). This is a process known as *sanctification*.

And as for our good works, we are able to keep God's commands only as a result of what He has already done and is continuing to do in us. That obedience is the *fruit* of what Jesus has given us—not the prerequisite to having a relationship with Him (1 John 3:18–20; also Gal. 5:22–23). In fact, the good works He calls us to accomplish are not even possible before He makes us His own and seals us with His Holy Spirit as a guarantee of our redemption forever (1 John 3:7, 24; also Eph. 1:13–14, 4:30).

When I saw this wonderful truth in seminary that day, I wanted to run around the classroom praising God! I finally saw what Philippians 1:6 promises: "He who began a good work in you will perfect it until the day of Christ Jesus." Our Savior is the One who finishes, guards, develops, and ensures the good work He's begun in us until we see Him face-to-face (Jude 24–25)!

> *Our obedience is the* fruit *of what Jesus has given us—not the prerequisite to having a relationship with Him.*

Undoubtedly, the truth I learned that day in seminary had a profound impact on my life. How did the Father use this to shape me?

FIRST, I REALIZED THAT NOT EVERYTHING ABOUT MY EARLY BELIEFS WAS WRONG. The church, like my dear mother, drilled into me the importance of obedience at an early age. Of course, I then had to recognize that this was not to earn my salvation but to align myself with God's will and position myself for the very best He has for my life. Instead of seeking the Father out of obligation, I learned to do so out of profound love and the joy of experiencing His presence. For that emphasis on submission to God I will always be grateful, because it has been the key to success at every crossroad of my life. Obedience always brings blessing. The Father has not always blessed me in the way I expected, but He has always provided exactly what I needed, when I needed it, and in the manner that helped me know He is indeed with me forever.

SECOND, THE TRUTH I LEARNED IN SEMINARY THAT DAY TAUGHT ME TO SEARCH SCRIPTURE THOROUGHLY AND TO TEST WHATEVER I HEAR, REGARDLESS OF HOW TRUSTWORTHY THE TEACHER IS. The believers in Berea were commended for this very practice. In Acts 17:11, they are called "noble-minded" because when they heard Paul preach, "they received the word with great eagerness, examining the Scriptures daily to see whether these things were so." They studied God's Word diligently and tested everything they were told, making sure that what they were hearing was true to what the Lord said and according to His will. It is incredibly important that we do the same, because if we don't, we may end up trapped in beliefs that continually cause us to experience defeat or self-condemnation, when what the Father really desires for us is a fruitful life filled with His power, freedom, and joy.

INTIMATELY DIRECTED

A final negative influence that shaped my path was that my mother remarried when I was nine years old. As I described in the previous chapter, I was left alone a great deal when I was young. This created all kinds of insecurities within me, and those inadequacies were exacerbated when my mother wed John Hall, a very negative, self-centered, and bitter man whom she'd met at the Dan River Textile Mill where she worked.

I had a terrible time understanding why Mother chose John; they were so opposite. She was petite, quiet, unhurried, and generous—a woman with a profound relationship with God. But John had unmanageable fits of rage. In fact, he was the angriest man I've ever known. Also, John was somewhat deaf, so when he spoke, he was *loud*. But worse than that, he spoke in a foul, jarring manner, and he never said a kind word. I can't recall him ever giving gifts or helping anyone. He told us he believed in God, but he rarely went to church or expressed anything that resembled trust in the Lord. On the contrary, he enjoyed making fun of my faith and often belittled my call to preach the gospel.

I suppose John wasn't that bad while they were dating, but he still wasn't a man I thought worthy of my mother. I later discovered that Becca's reason for being with him was—as was characteristic of everything else she did—selfless and sacrificial: She thought I needed a father figure. Sadly, I never saw John as anything like what I thought a dad should be.

But as is true in many abusive relationships, everything changed after Mother and John exchanged vows. From the beginning of their marriage, John brought a great deal of anger, conflict, and hostility into our once peaceful home, and it was often over very petty issues. I recall once having a terrible argument with him about the fried chicken we were having for dinner. It was as if he wasn't happy until everyone else in the house was as miserable as he was. He seemed compelled to be aggressive, faultfinding, and at times even violent—provoking us until a heated fight broke out.

I never felt safe around John, so I would sleep with my door locked and my hunting rifle by my side. But that didn't solve the real problem, which was that he was intolerably abusive toward my mother—verbally, emotionally, and even physically hurting her in ways that absolutely broke my heart. I couldn't stand it.

Of course, Mother couldn't bear it whenever he came after me. She was so loving and protective of me, she always intervened. Regrettably, that meant he would take whatever rage he felt toward me out on her and I cannot begin to express how deeply that grieved me.

Nonetheless, I still remember the first time he succeeded in striking me. I was fifteen, we were having dinner, and I made a comment. I don't remember what it was, but whatever I said triggered John's anger, and he slapped me across the face so forcefully it left me reeling. At that moment, something inside me snapped, and I punched him back as hard as I could. Thankfully, that did the job, and he never hit me again. But from then on, John made it exceedingly clear that he didn't like having me around. He wanted me out of the house as soon as possible, and I was glad to oblige him.

What good came from that situation? The first was the birth of my half sister, Susie, whom I have always loved dearly. She was born a couple of years before I left for college, so we didn't have as close a relationship as I would have liked in those early years. Fortunately, caring for our mother and our love for the Lord brought us together as we grew older.

God also used the friction between me and John in a positive way to build my intimate relationship with Him. Because of my stepfather's explosive behavior, I never felt completely safe walking into our home. I was never sure what he might do or what would set off his uncontrolled anger. So when John was in the house, I wanted to be out of it. This resulted in three positive developments.

First, it increased my prayer life exponentially because I spent a lot of time alone with God. After I finished school and delivering papers, I didn't want to go home. So I would go down to the church, and the janitor there—a wonderful man named Art— would let me in. I would head down to the basement area, go through three different doors, and shut myself in the quietest, darkest, most remote Sunday school classroom I could find. I loved it because I could pray all I wanted to—as loudly and for however long I needed to, just as I had learned to do in the Pentecostal Holiness Church. But down in that basement, it was just me and God, and I spent many very meaningful hours with Him without any distractions.

Likewise, in the spring and summer, I would take my .22 Winchester rifle, which had a great scope, and go shooting down by Fall Creek. I would walk along the banks or sit up on a beautiful green grassy hill overlooking the water and talk to God. I would ask Him to show me who

I could pray all I wanted to— as loudly and for however long I needed to.

He was, how I could know Him better, and what I could do to serve Him. I would seek His will about school and how to live my life. Those were very special times. I had such a hunger for the Lord to teach me the truth.

Interestingly, even though I was alone, I really never felt lonely there. With that rifle in my hand and God in my heart, I wasn't scared of anything. I had such a sense of security and courage because of the awesome oneness I felt with the Father.

SECOND, THAT EXPERIENCE MOTIVATED ME TO MAKE THE MOST OF MY NEWSPAPER BUSINESS—and as I've often said, God worked through that route in many ways.

First and foremost, of course, that job got me up and talking to my heavenly Father early in the morning. I usually got up at five o'clock to deliver the papers, and I would converse with the Lord all along the way. Those were wonderful times. I had such a real, abiding awareness that God heard me and cared for me when I talked to Him about things that were happening in my life. So I will always be grateful for the lifelong habit it formed in me.

Delivering papers also taught me about stewardship and gave me my first real spending money. I earned about $16 a week—enough to buy school lunches, books, clothes, and also to help my mother with some of the household expenses. I was also able to purchase suits and shoes for church. Suits in those days went for $29.95, with the really nice ones costing $34.95. So I bought them on layaway—putting a dollar down and then paying as much as I could every week until I reached the full price. This system allowed me to buy two new suits a year and look my very best for church.

Additionally, my route taught me about making wise investments. As I said previously, I began delivering the *Commercial Appeal* on Monday and Thursday mornings when I was thirteen. About a year later, I heard that a fellow who had a much larger route of our daily newspaper—the *Register and Bee*, which was close to where I lived— was going to give it up. So I went to talk to him and expressed my interest in taking it over. He told me he would sell the route to me for

$125. That seemed reasonable, so at the age of fourteen my stepfather and I went down to the bank and got a loan, which I paid back at a rate of $5 a week. I kept that route until I went off to college, and it taught me invaluable lessons about the importance of investing in my goals and dreams.

I also learned how to deal with people. Of course, I had my share of mean dogs, customers who refused to pay, and people who moved away without taking care of their bills. One lady owed me for two and a half weeks' worth of papers. She called her husband to come to the door, and he shoved me down the steps. That was an education in itself.

But I also learned good customer service. The *Commercial Appeal* held competitions for the delivery boys—challenging us to see who could enlist the most new customers or who received the fewest complaints in a specified period of time. I made it a point to win as many of those contests as I could, which meant I had to learn to be the very best paperboy I could be.

THIRD, IT WAS THROUGH MY PAPER ROUTE THAT I LEARNED THAT GOD WAS MY GREAT PROTECTOR. One morning, two strange men tried to kidnap me while I was out delivering papers. Thankfully, I got away from them and was able to tell my uncle, who was head of the detectives on the police force. I knew God was with me and had helped me survive their attempt to abduct me. I also knew that because I was able to report them immediately to my uncle, the police would be hot on their trail and would do everything they could to prevent them from harming other children.

Likewise, North Main Street in Danville was a major thoroughfare that I had to crisscross several times a day in order to complete my route. I recall numerous times when I stepped out into the street, only to have a car come to a screeching halt just inches away from me. Each time I was profoundly aware of God's awesome protection and provision. Because of that, I learned not to fear. I knew my life was in His good and faithful hands.

Of course, everything that the Lord taught me through that newspaper route would become very important as I learned to deliver another kind of news—the Good News of salvation through Jesus Christ. As a preacher of the gospel, I would need to continue making my intimate relationship with the Father my first priority every day. I would have to be a good steward

> *I learned not to fear. I knew my life was in His good and faithful hands.*

of all the resources He entrusted me with. It would be essential for me to invest wisely—both in projects and in others—in order to grow the kingdom of God. I would need to know how to deal with people—loving them, developing them, and helping them to become all that the Lord had created them to be. Finally, I would always have to count on the Father to be my Protector and Defender. Yes, my newspaper route taught me a great deal, indeed.

CALLED AND PREPARED

The point is that even during those very early years, adversity was a bridge that God used to draw me closer to Him and to shape me into the man and preacher He wanted me to become. He does the same for you. No one wants to experience hardships and afflictions. And the truth of the matter is that when they happen during our childhoods, they often become an excuse for us to give up, treat others badly, and be negative. But when trials arise, we have a choice about how to respond to them: as a burden or a bridge. We can see them as weights that depress us and keep us discouraged, or as conduits that the Lord works through to develop us into who He wants us to become and to deepen our intimate relationship with Him.

I knew from the time I knelt to ask Jesus into my heart at the age of twelve that I was meant to serve God with my life. In fact, the very next day, I tried to lead my friend Leon Henderson to Christ, but he said, "I'm too young for that now. One of these days I'll think about it, but I'm going to wait until I get older before I do that." I was devastated. I just wanted Leon to enjoy the freedom and excitement I felt when I accepted Jesus as my Savior. In fact, I longed for everyone to experience it.

But this calling was not something I totally understood or knew how to verbalize as a twelve-year-old. I've often told the story of how my best friend in high school, Raymond Barber, and I sat on the ball field one evening when we were both fourteen years old. Raymond was Baptist and I was still attending the Pentecostal Holiness Church, but we were great friends because we both loved the Lord so deeply.

I asked him, "Raymond, what are you going to do when you grow up?"

He said, "I don't know. What are you going to do?"

I said, "I don't know." We later confessed to each other that we both had been called to preach at that point but were too scared to say it out loud. This was not because we didn't have role models. We did. Raymond's father was the pastor of the Baptist Tabernacle, which was the largest church in Danville at the time. He was a very influential man in the community and even had a successful radio program. And of course, I had my godly mother and other people I could talk to about what the Lord was telling me.

It is just that when a person is called to serve God with his or her life, it takes time to process what it all means because it is such a deep, integral part of who we are. As Paul tells us in 2 Corinthians 5:14, "The love of Christ controls us." Or as the New International Version translates it, "Christ's love compels us." When you are called to ministry, you're motivated to do it—you almost can't do otherwise. God points your life in the direction of serving Him, and nothing else fits or seems right.

There never was a time when I audibly heard the Lord say to me, "I want you to preach." But as I indicated earlier, from the moment I was saved, I didn't think about doing or being anything else. I simply came to the realization that preaching the gospel was what I was created to do.

My son, Andy, would later ask me, "Did you ever consider being anything other than a preacher?" I really never did. The only other occupation that even came close to drawing my attention was that I was always fascinated by bands and orchestras. Although the only instrument I ever played was the drums in college, I have always been captivated by the way so many talented musicians can gather with their different instruments and make such beautiful music together. It seems effortless and enchanting. The only person in such concerts not playing an instrument was the conductor, and I would often think to myself, *That would be a fun job to have.* To look out for all the different instruments—understanding their challenges, potential, and the way they interacted—and to be able to lead them in the manner that would best help them? That sounded wonderful to me.

But of course, that's what a preacher does. He looks at his church and leads it by proclaiming the Word of God faithfully—navigating

> *When you are called to ministry, you're motivated to do it—you almost can't do otherwise.*

the obstacles, guiding people to where they are spiritually gifted, and keeping everyone focused on the goal of glorifying Christ. And from the time I was a small boy, the Father used everything in my life to prepare me for that goal—to help me lead congregations in overtures of obedience fit for heaven.

For example, I was a boy during World War II, and I remember learning about the precariousness of life in a very powerful way. Near my home was a boardinghouse run by a woman named Mrs. Johnson. The wives of soldiers would stay there while their husbands fought overseas.

Every evening, those dear ladies gathered around the radio to listen to Gabriel Heatter's reports about the ongoing battles. They would pray for his comforting assurance, "There is good news tonight." But often, their tears would flow as reports of losses, defeats, and casualties were transmitted over the airwaves.

The war took its toll on many in our community. As those anxious days passed, families' worst fears would be confirmed and gold stars would appear in windows throughout the town—announcing the sad news that another loved one had been lost. Those families knew firsthand the incredible cost of safeguarding our nation and our liberty.

As a child, I saw how brave and determined these ladies and families were in the face of such adversity. At the same time, I recognized the fragility of life and how quickly someone's world can change. I realized the absolute urgency of preaching the gospel and the courage I would need to do so unfailingly, regardless of the enemies that might rise up. That experience built in me a desire to express with my life and lead others to express with their lives the beautiful lines in "The Battle Hymn of the Republic" by Julia Ward

Howe. These words have accompanied so many brave soldiers as they marched out to do combat:

> *In the beauty of the lilies Christ was born across the sea,*
> *With a glory in His bosom that transfigures you and me.*
> *As He died to make men holy, let us live to make men free,*
> *While God is marching on.*

HOW GOD HAS SHAPED YOU

More than likely, you experienced life-changing hardships when you were young, and you are probably facing some difficult trials today as well. The question is: How are you responding to the adverse circumstances of your life? Have you permitted them to embitter you and shape your life in a negative way? Have you allowed them to convince you that you are inadequate, incapable, unworthy, or unlovable? Or are you asking God to work through them to develop your character and deepen your intimate relationship with Him? Are you trying to handle your trials on your own, using your limited resources, turning to your friends for advice, escaping into hobbies or addictions—but still facing defeat over and over again? Or have you invited the Father to transform your afflictions into a stepping-stone to victory?

Have you invited the Father to transform your afflictions into a stepping-stone to victory?

I can guarantee that when it comes to the challenges you've faced and are currently enduring, your human coping mechanisms will ultimately fail you. Your adversity will become an overwhelming

burden. But if you turn to Jesus, He will show you how every en-
cumbrance and pain can become an avenue of His glory, purpose, and
grace. So I pray that you will choose to see all of the difficult circumstances you've experienced as a bridge to a deeper relationship with
Jesus. As a believer, the awesome power of the Holy Spirit can equip
and transform you through any suffering you could ever face and
bring you to a place of indescribable intimacy with our precious Lord
and Savior, Jesus Christ. And that, my friend, is absolutely awesome.

3

Foundational Influences

Faith of our fathers, we will love
Both friend and foe in all our strife;
And preach Thee, too, as love knows how
By kindly words and virtuous life.
—Frederick W. Faber, 1849

"Obey God and leave all the consequences to Him."
—George Washington Stanley

The calling I talked about in the last chapter became very real to me as I contemplated what God was leading me to do with my life. Even as a teenager, I was very serious about Christ. I truly wanted Jesus to be my Lord—I longed to do what was pleasing to Him and to be in the center of His will. And He gave me plenty of opportunities and people to help me express that longing. But almost immediately it became apparent that I would have to be very careful in choosing whom I would allow to influence me. As Proverbs 13:20 teaches us, "He who walks with wise men will be wise, but the companion of fools will suffer harm."

If we spend time with people who are walking with the Lord, it helps us to grow closer to Him. The company we keep influences how we view the situations and circumstances of our lives. On the other hand, when we fail to fellowship with strong believers, we will almost surely drift away from our heavenly Father.

WALKING AWAY FROM THE UNWISE

One day this principle came into sharp focus for me. I was sixteen and was meeting a group of seven friends whom I had been close to for many years. We had enjoyed many fun times together at church events, exploring the nearby woods, and skating. On this particular night, we followed our usual practice of gathering at the local drugstore, which was about a mile away from where I lived. We'd hang out there for a while, have some chocolate shakes, and then figure out what we would do for the rest of the evening. I had gotten my mother to press my trousers so I'd look my best.

Now, my friends were good fellows, and I knew they loved God. But in the course of the conversation, one of them suggested going over to the local pool hall and checking it out. Unfortunately, in those days, pool halls were really beer joints—known primarily for their drinking, gambling, and carousing. Of course, the guys swore that they wouldn't have any alcohol and assured me that no one would ever know that we'd been there. But instantly I knew that my friends were going down a bad path and that I was facing a life-impacting decision.

Would I go with the guys in order to maintain the friendships that had always been so important to me? Or would I obey the inner promptings of the Holy Spirit, who was saying loudly and clearly, "Don't go!"?

I'm sure I hesitated for a moment because I cared for my friends deeply. But in my heart, I knew the answer. So I said, "No, I don't think so. I'm not going to do that. I'm going home."

And then I walked away.

I won't say it was easy, because it wasn't—not by a long shot. As you know, I struggled terribly with loneliness, and in that moment, I felt awfully alone. But that feeling of alienation did not last long. As I walked up that solitary dark street, the Lord spoke to my heart in the most powerful way. I know exactly where I was—715 North Main Street, at R. B. Rogers's house. I knew it so well because Mr. Rogers was one of the customers on my newspaper route.

But right there, in front of Mr. Rogers's home, the Father said to me clearly, "You will never regret this decision." And the truth of the matter is, I never have.

Sure, things were never the same between me and those friends, and that was a painful reality. But if I'd listened to them, I'm not sure what would have happened or how I would have hurt my testimony. But I know that by submitting to God in that instance, I took an important step forward in my faith.

I know that by submitting to God in that instance, I took an important step forward in my faith.

UNEQUALLY YOKED

The same was true when I faced my first big crisis in prayer, which, like for most young men, was because of a girl. I was dating a young lady by the name of Barbara Ann Johnson, whom I had known since the first grade, when Mother and I lived in the basement of her father's grocery business. She wasn't my first girlfriend—I'd had two others before her—but she was the most serious one I had during my early years. We began seeing each other in junior high and continued until I was a senior in college.

Barbara Ann and I went through quite a lot together. One night, I borrowed her father's car to take her on a date. Unfortunately, that evening, the roads were very slick. We rounded a particularly dangerous corner, and before I knew it, the car flipped over several times. I remember thinking, *This must be a dream. This can't possibly be real.*

Miraculously, when the car came to a stop, neither of us was hurt.

A witness rushed over and pulled us out of the wreck, making sure we were okay and that we got home safely. Of course, what worried us most was what her father would say. But Mr. Johnson was a gracious man, and he was very grateful that we were all right. All he asked of us was that we each pay $75 toward repairing the car.

That kind of near-death experience often bonds people forever. But as the end of my college years drew near, I prayed about whether or not to continue dating Barbara Ann. It was time to make a decision about where our relationship was going, and as I said, it created quite a crisis for me. I really cared for Barbara Ann. She was sweet, caring, and beautiful—the kind of girl any fellow would be blessed to have as a girlfriend or wife. But whenever I was with her, I felt like there was something missing, and I struggled to identify what it was.

Thankfully, as I prayed, the problem became very apparent— Barbara Ann simply wasn't spiritually focused. I planned to serve God for the rest of my life, and He made it clear that I would need someone by my side who would do so as well, who was willing to listen to the Holy Spirit and make the sacrifices that the ministry would require. It was difficult, but I ended my relationship with Barbara Ann and looked forward to the woman the Father had set apart just for me.

Of course, making choices about whom we allow to influence our life is never easy. We grow to care for people, and it is natural to want their respect, acceptance, and loyalty—even when it costs us dearly. Certainly, that is how Jesus loves us—it was extremely costly for Him to empty Himself, taking the form of a bond-servant and laying

> *Any friendship or association that hinders our relationship with God is far from a good idea.*

down His life for us on the cross (Phil. 2:5–11). But there is a limit to what we can and should sacrifice. And the truth of the matter is that any friendship or association that hinders our relationship with God is far from a good idea.

A SPIRITUAL FATHER

Thankfully, the Lord put some truly wonderful influences in my life. For example, I listened to the Baptist evangelist Charles E. Fuller on the *Old Fashioned Revival Hour* on the radio Sunday afternoons. I never missed his program. I was eager to hear him and the other great preachers and to learn all the priceless biblical principles they were teaching. I also wanted God to speak to me like He had spoken to them.

Likewise, I have already described how my mother was such an extraordinary example and how she helped me grow in my faith and service to God. Of course, Mother never told me what to do in regard to my calling. She never said she wanted me to be a preacher or go into the ministry. Instead, she simply encouraged me to get on my knees before the Father and ask Him to show me very clearly what

He wanted me to do. She would say, "If God is calling you to preach, obey Him and trust Him to make you into the very best preacher you can be." She was always so wise.

There was also a dear man in those early days named Craig Stowe, who served as my Sunday school teacher at the Pentecostal Holiness Church and had a great impact on my life. He was an incredible man of faith whom I loved dearly and who inspired me profoundly.

Craig was truly a man of God both in word and deed. He told a story of being in the U.S. Navy during World War II. The enemy was advancing, and the crew of his ship were readying themselves for the impending attack. Someone had to go up on the crow's nest—which was dizzyingly high on the mainmast—to stand watch for inbound adversarial forces. Of course, not only was that post incredibly far off the ground and therefore terrifying for those with a fear of heights, but it also offered little protection against incoming fire. Anyone up there would be very vulnerable indeed. So as the sailors lined up for duty, they were asked to volunteer for the fearsome responsibility. As might be expected, no one came forward.

But Craig said that in that moment the Lord spoke to him clearly and assured him, "Craig, I'm with you just as much up there as I am down here. You can do it." So Craig stepped out in faith and agreed to take on the dangerous task. Though the attack was fierce and many men were lost, Craig came through the entire ordeal without even a scratch. He told us, "Nothing ever came anywhere near me. God protected me, just as He promised."

That was the type of man Craig Stowe was—full of faith and very courageous. But that was only one side of him. What actually affected me most about Craig was how exceedingly kind he was. He had a sweet, wonderful spirit. He called me by name every Sunday and always had a good word. About once a week, as I delivered newspapers up and down North Main Street, he would pull up in his car and buy a paper from me—always giving me more than it cost and insisting I keep the change. Craig would ask how I was doing, show interest in my life, and without fail say, "Charles, I just want you to know I've been thinking about you and I pray for you often." It was a practice he continued even long after I left the Pentecostal Holiness Church and he was no longer my Sunday school teacher. He still stopped, bought a paper, and told me he cared.

It wasn't until later that it occurred to me that Craig didn't need to buy a newspaper from me because he already had one delivered to his home. But he did so in order to create an opportunity to talk to me and influence my young heart. That was his character—always looking for ways to bring joy into people's lives and express the love of God to others. He was a great and steady source of encouragement to me when I was a boy, and he ended up being the closest I've ever had to an earthly father.

What actually affected me most about Craig was how exceedingly kind he was.

Seventy years later, I still thank God for Craig Stowe. He was the only man I can remember during those early years who truly showed he cared for me, and I am so grateful I will see him again in heaven. I will always hold on to the story of how the Lord was with him up on that crow's nest, because it reminds me that God will always be with me, too—regardless of where I am. And I will always remember the kindness he showed me when he stopped to talk to me. He demonstrated how crucial it is to use those priceless moments to tell others how important they are to us and in God's eyes. That's a legacy any godly man would be proud of.

A LIFE-CHANGING HERITAGE

Another man who influenced me profoundly was one whom you've no doubt heard me talk about before—my grandfather, George Washington Stanley. Granddad was a fiery, Spirit-filled Pentecostal preacher, so as I contemplated my future as a minister of the gospel, I had a strong desire to spend time with him and learn from his experiences. Consequently, in my senior year of high school, I wrote to him and made plans to see him.

I knew only a little about my granddad prior to visiting him for an amazing six days in 1949. When I was nine years old, I spent some time with him and had the privilege of hearing him preach a full week of revival messages. He was a quiet and easygoing man, but when he got to preaching, there was no stopping him. He was absolutely on fire, bold, fervent, and courageous for the Lord. The Spirit of God shook that small Pentecostal church and the people there prayed loudly and long after he was done giving the message. God worked through him in an awesome way. I was able to visit my grandfather again when I was twelve, and it was just as wonderful. I knew that what he saying and how he was preaching were somehow becoming part of me.

So my entire understanding of Granddad when I packed my bags and set out to see him came through those two visits and what he said in those sermons—and it was more than enough. In my mind, my grandfather was like Moses—tall, skinny, old, and exceedingly wise. More than anything I wanted to find out how he was able talk to God so well. I was confident that if anyone could offer me wisdom about serving the Lord with my life, he certainly could.

So at sixteen, I got on an old Trailways bus and made my way to Siler City, North Carolina, and to my grandfather's house at the edge of town. He was about seventy years old and had retired from preaching, but something about him still carried that indescribable quality of the great men of God—you could tell that he had been in the Lord's presence and that the Holy Spirit was overflowing in him.

He told me he still enjoyed doing some farming in his backyard, and he showed me his wonderful garden—full of corn, tomatoes, butterbeans, and other vegetables. Even at seventy, he used a plow, which he had to push on his own. His face was tanned from the sun, and his hands showed the marks of a man who believed he would reap what he sowed. I'm certain he had many a wonderful conversation with the Father as he tended to his fields and harvested his crops. I couldn't wait to learn from him.

So for the next six days, Granddad and I sat out on his screened-in back porch and just talked. I asked him endless questions about his life and ministry, and he patiently answered. I just kept thinking, *This is the most spiritual person I've ever talked to.* He impacted my life profoundly. I was like a sponge, soaking up everything he said. In fact, I believe that those were six of the most important days of my life, because they absolutely revolutionized the way I would live and serve the Lord. The stories my grandfather told me became etched on my heart and formed the five guiding principles that have shaped my path ever since:

> *Granddad's face was tanned from the sun, and his hands showed the marks of a man who believed he would reap what he sowed.*

1. The most important thing in your life is your relationship with God.

2. Obey God, and leave all the consequences to Him.
3. God will move heaven and earth to reveal His will to you if you really want to know it and do it.
4. God will provide for all your needs.
5. God will protect you.

FIRST, THE MOST IMPORTANT THING IN YOUR LIFE IS YOUR RELA-TIONSHIP WITH GOD. Of course, the first thing my grandfather said was how crucial it is to be rightly related to God through His Son Jesus. He confided that as a young man he started his ministry feeling very inadequate because he didn't have much education—he'd only made it to the sixth grade. In fact, he learned to read by studying the Bible. And he picked up how to preach by crying out to the Father and asking Him what to say.

This was extremely encouraging to me because of the inadequacies and fears I was struggling with. To think that such a great man of God had them as well gave me hope that the Lord could make something out of my life, too. And what this ultimately showed me was the amazing way the Savior can work through any simple but willing servant who is completely committed to Him. As 2 Chronicles 16:9 reminds us, "The eyes of the LORD move to and fro throughout the earth that He may strongly support those whose heart is completely His."

This is why I often say, "Our intimacy with God is His highest priority for our lives because it determines the impact of our lives." The more profound our fellowship with the Father, the more powerful our lives—regardless of whether we're educated, attractive, wealthy, or of a prominent social standing. We don't have to be perfect, not by any means. No, it is our relationship with God that makes all the difference in our lives—our love for Him, our willingness to serve Him, and our dependence upon His Holy Spirit.

So how did my grandfather achieve such a deep and transformative relationship with the Lord? Much like my mother did:

First, he spent a great deal of time meditating on Scripture. He didn't just read the Word; he also asked questions, such as: "God, what are You saying to me? How does this apply to my life? What are You trying to correct? How do You want me to respond to You in obedience?"

The second thing he did was become a person of prayer. Grandfather didn't just go before the throne of grace at night before he went to bed or when he was in trouble. Instead, he took the apostle Paul's commands to heart: "Devote yourselves to prayer" (Col. 4:2) and "pray without ceasing" (1 Thess. 5:17). This meant that his life was one long conversation with God—in which he shared all the joys of life as well as the sorrows.

Third, as with any good relationship, my grandfather realized how important it was to actively listen to the Savior. Granddad was keenly aware that he was the servant of God, not the other way around. If he wanted a deep relationship with the Lord that would bring him into unified oneness with Him, he would have to train his ears to hear Him. And if he truly desired to have God's direction, wisdom, and power, he would have to pay close attention to what the Father was saying.

MY GRANDDAD'S SECOND GUIDING PRINCIPLE WAS THAT WE OBEY GOD AND LEAVE ALL THE CONSEQUENCES TO HIM. Of course, this led me to ask Granddad, "How do you know for certain when God has spoken to you?" He told me that I would have a profound awareness in my heart of how He was leading me. Then he said, "But Charles, always remember this: You obey God no matter what." This brought us to this second principle—which was one of the most significant things my grandfather shared—the commitment to absolute obedience to whatever the Lord commanded. As James 1:22 (NLT) admonishes, "Don't just listen to God's word. You must do what it says."

Granddad told me, "Charles, if God tells you to run your head through a brick wall, you head for the wall, and when you get there, God will make a hole for it." We both chuckled when he said it, but I knew he meant it with all of his heart. Granddad was completely fearless, which was evident in how he preached the truth and never considered compromising what he believed. He had such a deep trust in and reverence for God that he couldn't imagine contradicting what the Lord said. This, of course, got him in trouble early on.

Granddad told me, "Charles, if God tells you to run your head through a brick wall, you head for the wall, and when you get there, God will make a hole for it."

You see, my grandfather had been attending a Methodist church when God called him to preach. As he studied Scripture, he came to the conclusion that once you're truly saved, you don't sin anymore—a concept known as "entire sanctification," which was consistent with the teachings of John Wesley and the early Holiness movement. Although I really wish my grandfather had been right that we would never again sin as believers, I don't actually agree with him on this point. I believe that sanctification is a process and that we will continue to struggle with the flesh as long as we're alive, a concept I spoke about briefly in chapter 2. This does not disqualify us from the grace of God; it acts as a constant reminder of how much we truly need Jesus (Rom. 7:14–24).

But because Granddad preached entire sanctification, that Methodist church expelled him from their fellowship. Likewise, other churches in the area wouldn't allow him to preach from their pulpits. One congregation after another rejected him, causing him to doubt the calling he had received.

Did that dissuade him? No. Did he water down the message so that he would have a place to preach or an income from a church? No. Although Granddad was disheartened for a time, he never gave up, he kept on serving God. Moreover, my grandfather went on to plant many churches in Virginia and North Carolina—including the Pentecostal Holiness Church in Danville where I accepted Jesus as my Savior.

He was an incredible example in regard to absolute obedience, and this principle has become a foundational cornerstone and anchor for my life: *Obey God and leave all the consequences to Him.* It's a phrase you've undoubtedly heard me repeat often. You do what the Lord tells you to do regardless of the circumstances or dangers you face, and you trust Him to make a path for you where there appears to be no way through.

We see this principle over and over again in the lives of the biblical saints—men such as Abraham, Moses, Daniel, and Paul.

- The Lord told Abraham to leave his home in Ur of the Chaldeans and every source of security he knew (Gen. 12:1–4). So at the age of seventy-five, with astounding faith in God, Abraham set out not knowing where he was going or what he would find when he got there (Heb. 11:8).

- God instructed Moses to take his shepherd's staff and be the conduit He would work through to deliver more than two million enslaved Israelites from Egypt, the most powerful empire on earth at the time (Ex. 3; Heb. 11:24–29). Moses had no armies or resources to help him, only the promises and presence of the Lord.
- The Father moved Daniel to continue praying to Him, even though doing so meant being thrown into the lions' den and certain death (Dan. 6:1–13).
- And the Savior called Paul to leave behind everything that constituted his confidence, identity, and status in order to spread the gospel throughout the known world (Acts 9:15–16; Phil. 3:4–9).

We cannot and should not forget that obedience to the Father has been and continues to be costly and will always require great courage from us. It certainly was for each and every one of the faithful biblical saints. But it is always worth it.

Because of their obedience:

- Abraham obtained the promise of becoming the father of many nations (Rom. 4:18–21).
- By God's provision and power, Moses led the people of Israel out of Egypt and to the Promised Land (Deut. 26:6–9).
- Daniel survived the lions' den and became a testimony of God's power to King Darius of Medo-Persia (Dan. 6:20–28).
- And Paul faithfully proclaimed the gospel, planting churches throughout Europe and Asia Minor and writing half of the books in the New Testament. Paul was able to proclaim with joy, "I have fought the good fight, I have finished the course,

I have kept the faith; in the future there is laid up for me the crown of righteousness, which the LORD, the righteous Judge, will award to me on that day; and not only to me, but also to all who have loved His appearing" (2 Tim. 4:7–8).

You never go wrong by obeying God. But you will always regret it when you don't trust Him.

THE THIRD GUIDING PRINCIPLE GRANDDAD SHARED WITH ME WAS THAT GOD WILL MOVE HEAVEN AND EARTH TO REVEAL HIS WILL TO YOU IF YOU REALLY WANT TO KNOW IT AND DO IT. Of course, no one likes rejection, and the truth of the matter is that a very long time passed without any open doors for my grandfather to preach. As you can imagine, he felt as if no one wanted him and wondered if he was somehow disqualified from the ministry God had called him to.

He told me that he really struggled during that time. If the Lord had called him into the ministry, why were there so many obstacles and difficulties? Why wasn't the Father providing a place from which he could serve? He wrestled with those questions for a long time. Then, one night, he was walking along an unpaved road and became so distraught that he just fell to his knees and cried out, "God, this seems impossible! If You're really calling me to preach and You're going to show me what to do, I need some evidence. Please, let me see a star fall." He wanted to be absolutely sure that his calling was real. Granddad said right at that moment he looked up, and two stars rocketed across the darkened celestial expanse.

It was the confirmation he needed—corroborated in a manner that could be engineered only by the omnipotent hand of the eternal, Almighty God.

This account would become very important for me some years later in college. My senior year at the University of Richmond was a particularly difficult season. Everything was going wrong, and I was absolutely miserable.

It was the confirmation he needed—corroborated in a manner that could be engineered only by the omnipotent hand of the eternal, Almighty God.

First, I was playing football on the Air Force ROTC team, and when I jumped up to catch a pass, I fell and tore a ligament in my leg. It was incredibly painful. I tried to muscle through it, but it got worse and worse. Finally, a friend convinced me to see a doctor, who put me in a heavy cast that stretched all the way from my thigh to my ankle. I had to wear it for several weeks, which frustrated me to no end because it made it nearly impossible to walk on the university's hilly campus carrying books.

What was even more exasperating was the liberalism espoused in my classes. For example, I had a philosophy instructor who claimed to teach the Bible, but he didn't believe in Jesus' resurrection. He actually made fun of Christ's deity. I had another professor who proclaimed that Mahatma Gandhi was just as divine as the Lord Jesus. I thought, *What in the world is this heresy? What is the point of wasting my time on this?* Of course, it all drove me to the Word to defend my convictions. But I still couldn't believe this was what comprised "excellence in education."

Moreover, when exam week arrived, I received a fifty on a trigonometry test and seventy-five on one in history. This was especially terrible because history was my major! I was a senior, and it seemed I'd spent years in school just to fail. So after dinner, I went back to my dorm room, got out my Bible and hymnal, and cried out to the

Lord. I prayed, "Father, I could fail to graduate here at the very end. Please help me." I was desperate to know God's plan and purpose for my life, but I felt as if He had completely walked out on me—as if He was utterly gone from my life. Heaven was silent. It was a truly terrible week.

At one point, the pressure grew so great that I went to visit some friends in Thomas Hall—Jim Brinkley and John Booth, who were from my hometown. I shared my struggle with them, and they prayed with me for a long while. Still, nothing happened.

I walked back to my dorm room at B-17 Jeter Hall utterly discouraged. As I approached the building, I looked up and saw that the light was on in my prayer partner Bond Harris's room. So I crawled in his open window and asked him to pray with me—which he did until about 1 a.m.

Still, I had no answers, and the heaviness I felt was unbearable.

I said, "Lord, I've got to be absolutely sure of what Your will is for me. I've prayed, pleaded, begged, and fasted. I've done everything I know to do. Father, please do *something*—my whole future is based on You. I want to serve You. Am I on the right track? Please show me what to do."

It was then that the Lord brought my grandfather's story about the falling stars to mind. I thought, *If Granddad asked God for something that specific and the Father answered him, then maybe He will do the same for me.* After all, my grandfather had many of the same doubts I was having, and the Lord used him in a wonderful way for His kingdom. Maybe He was working the same way in my life.

So I prayed, "God, I know I don't have any business asking You this, but if this is Your will for my life—if You are really calling me to preach—please let me see two falling stars like my grandfather did." I stared up into the sky for a long time—two lines of tall pine trees on either side and the bright Milky Way in the middle. It was a stunning sight, but no falling stars.

A couple of evenings later, my friend Avery Witcher, who was also from Danville, invited me to walk up to West Hampton Village to get a hamburger. We headed for town and had our dinner. On the way back, Avery said, "Hey, Charles, I know a shortcut back to the dorm. Follow me." He led me around to Saint Stephen's Episcopal Church's backyard. About halfway across it, he stopped, looked up at the amazing view, and said, "Isn't it a beautiful night?"

Well, I was so discouraged, I didn't care too much about how lovely the evening sky appeared, but I peered up all the same. At that moment, two luminous meteors shot like arrows across the dark expanse at the same time.

Avery said, "Wow! Did you see that?"

Unmoved, I said, "Yes, I saw them," but strangely, I didn't think much of it.

It wasn't until I got back to my room in the dorm and I was brushing my teeth that God spoke to my heart, *What did you ask Me for?*

I replied, "Well, Lord, I've seen a falling star before."

Two at the same time?

"No."

That's right, you haven't. You've never seen that before because you've never requested it until now. You asked Me, and I've answered your prayer.

I fell on my face and thanked God with all my heart. It occurred to me that if Avery hadn't taken me to that new shortcut through the Episcopal churchyard, I would have walked down the street with the traffic lights blinding my view and might never have seen those two meteors. I had no doubt in my mind that the Father's providential hand was guiding me. Just as He had with my grandfather, He settled the issue of my calling once and for all. God had moved heaven and earth to confirm His will.

THE FOURTH GUIDING PRINCIPLE I LEARNED FROM MY GRANDDAD WAS THAT GOD WILL PROVIDE FOR ALL YOUR NEEDS. Still, knowing the Lord's will and being committed to it does not ensure an easy life. Even though my grandfather was certain he was called to preach, he had nowhere to do so for a long time. So he kept seeking the Father's direction, and eventually God showed him he could hold his revival meetings in a tent as others had done. Of course, tent revivals and camp meetings had been around since the late 1700s because of American expansion into the frontier territories. Church buildings had not yet been constructed in the new settlements, so preachers would gather people wherever they could to proclaim the Word of God. During Granddad's time, revivals in tents had become especially popular among Pentecostal and Holiness preachers because they could move around and not be tied down to one place. And so my grandfather got the idea that he could do the same.

Granddad's only problem was that he had no money and therefore could not afford to purchase a tent, which cost about $300 at the time. So George Washington Stanley did what any of us would do—he got a job. With little schooling and no occupational training, Granddad did the menial work that was available, which was cutting railroad ties for the local lines. He chopped down trees, trimmed them to size, and earned twenty cents for each eight-foot tie he created, which was only a few each day. It was a very rough business for very little pay.

Knowing the Lord's will and being committed to it does not ensure an easy life.

In fact, there was a saying back then that hacking ties was "a hard way to serve the Lord." It was certainly true, even for turn-of-the-century workers who were accustomed to difficult physical labor. Sadly, after several months of storing up every penny, Granddad had managed to save only $40, a far cry from the amount he needed to purchase the tent. Obviously, it would be a very long time before he could afford one. My grandfather told me that at that point he felt he'd never get around to preaching. Hacking ties was wearing him out, and the $300 seemed further away than ever. Of course, in the 1920s that was an enormous amount of money.

But my grandfather didn't give up, and he had faith that the Lord would eventually provide what he needed in one way or another. Granddad prayed, "Father, You called me to preach and know how much money I need for a tent. This is the best I can do, but I know You will help me." Of course, the Lord loves that kind of faith. While he was praying, Granddad had a vision of a little house on a corner, with rosebushes in front and a white picket fence around it. He recognized it as a place he had seen during a visit to a little town not very far away, but he could not recall how to get to it.

The next day, Granddad went into that town and walked up and down the streets, but he couldn't find the house. Again, he was moved to his knees in prayer. After he arose, he looked up, saw the house in the distance, and knew that if he went there, God would provide for his needs. So Granddad went up to the house and knocked on the door, completely unsure about what he was supposed to say.

To his surprise, the lady who answered exclaimed, "Why, Mr. Stanley! I've been hoping to talk to you. I have something for you." She invited him in and retrieved a small brown-paper sack. She handed it to him and said, "God told me to give you this." He thanked her, chatted with her for a while, and then left.

When he opened the bag, he found three hundred $1 bills—exactly what he needed to buy the tent. He told me that's when he learned to always trust God, wait for Him to work, and know for certain He will take full responsibility for all our needs when we obey Him.

Thankfully, I remembered what my grandfather said about the Lord's provision when I was in my third year of college and got down to just ten cents in funds. All I had to my name was one dime. I can still recall looking at that shiny little coin in the palm of my hand and realizing how very small it was compared to all the needs I had.

But I thought about Granddad and I prayed, "God, You provided for my grandfather in such a powerful way. I only have ten cents left, and You know how much my housing and classes cost. You've brought me this far, and You know my heart is devoted to You. I'm going to trust You to help me." I then went on my way, hopeful for God's intervention.

That day, after my classes were done, I went by the post office. There in my box was a letter from Mrs. Johnson, the lady who was my neighbor in Danville. I used to mow her lawn and liked her well enough, but she had never written to me or tried to contact me before, so I was very curious to read her note. She wrote that for some reason she felt a strong conviction about sending me some money, so she was enclosing a check for $25 and prayed it would bless me. Boy, did it ever!

Mrs. Johnson couldn't possibly have known the wonderful reassurance the Father would give me through her gift. The Lord had provided for me powerfully, just as He had for my grandfather. And because of it, I gained even more confidence about His calling on my life.

THE FINAL GUIDING PRINCIPLE I LEARNED FROM GRANDDAD WAS THAT GOD WILL PROTECT YOU. One after another, Granddad told me stories that inspired my faith and helped me trust God. But there was one more tale he would tell that would shape how I responded to a different aspect of ministry—how to fight my battles.

My grandfather recounted a time when two inebriated men came into the church on a Sunday morning while he was preaching and sat down among the members of his congregation. They smelled of alcohol and made a terrible fuss—making rude comments, joking inappropriately, and distracting the rest of the people from the message with their antics. My grandfather tried to be patient, because they obviously needed Jesus. But they were so rowdy, he had no choice but to say, "You either shut up or get out." That stunned them for a moment. But after a minute or two, they surprisingly got up and walked out.

After the service, Granddad was shaking hands and conversing with people as was his custom, when two of the deacons came rushing up to him and said, "Those two drunks are outside, and they've gotten themselves some butcher knives. They told us that they're planning to kill you. We've got to call the police."

He replied, "No, I don't want you to call the police. I want you to go home." They tried to convince Granddad to change his mind and call the authorities, but he wouldn't. They begged him to let them stay and help him, but he refused and insisted that they go. He was resolute—God would protect him. Reluctantly, the two deacons left him.

It was then that my grandfather took his well-worn *Thompson Chain-Reference Bible* and knelt down at the altar. He simply prayed, "God I'm preaching for You. I know I am in Your care, and I'm trusting You to show Yourself mighty in this situation." Then he got up, put that old Bible next to his heart, and walked out the front door of the church. Sure enough, those two fellows were at the bottom of the steps. But as my grandfather advanced in their direction, they froze in their tracks, and he was able to walk right in between them without any problems.

Granddad went home and sat down to eat Sunday dinner with his family. Suddenly they began to hear sirens in the distance, which was very odd in the small rural town of Siler City. So my grandfather got up and rushed toward the sound of the commotion a couple of blocks away. It turned out that those two men had driven their automobile into a light pole, and one of the live electrical wires had torn loose, striking the car and setting it ablaze. Regrettably, both men burned to death.

"God, I know I am in Your care, and I'm trusting You to show Yourself mighty in this situation."

That was a sad story with a terrible ending, of course, but through it God spoke directly to my spirit: *Trust Me to be your Protector.* It immediately reminded me of a time when one of my neighbors—a bitter lady who was usually out of sorts—was in a particularly foul mood. I don't know what I did that made her so angry, but she got out her .22 rifle and shot at me. The bullet came so close, I heard it go by my ear. We eventually found it lodged in the wall of a friend's house behind where I was standing. The Lord was certainly my Shield and Defender that day—and has been ever since.

Because of my grandfather's testimony, I've always trusted the Father to safeguard me. Of course there were many conflicts after my visit with him in which this principle would guide my conduct. I'll tell you about several of them in the remaining chapters. But in each and every instance, I knew that I would not have to fight or defend myself; rather, I could count on God to help me. As Isaiah 54:17 promises, " 'No weapon that is formed against you will prosper;

and every tongue that accuses you in judgment you will condemn. This is the heritage of the servants of the LORD, and their vindication is from Me,' declares the LORD." Which is why I always say, "Fight your battles on your knees and you'll win every time."

WHO IS INFLUENCING YOU?

The point is that my relationships with my mother, Craig Stowe, and my grandfather shaped my life in an incredibly important way that cannot be underestimated. They not only showed me practical aspects of the Christian life that would keep me on course through every mountain and valley, but also the kind of person I wanted to become. I knew that if God worked in such a powerful way in their lives, I could absolutely trust Him to work in mine, too.

How about you? Have you chosen relationships that build your faith and strengthen your Christian life? Or do those closest to you consistently tear you down and weaken your trust in God? Make sure that you are choosing your spiritual mentors and friends wisely.

How can you do so? Analyze your relationships. Good influences:

1. *Drive you*—motivating you to be and do your best in every area. So look at the person's life. Does he have a godly character that inspires you to seek God more? Does being around him build your faith and confidence in the Lord? Or do that individual's words and actions lead you away from your relationship with Jesus—even subtly? Everyone you know will either move you toward the Father or away from Him, so be very careful about whom you choose to be closest to you.

2. *Develop you*—causing you to mature in your faith and become

the person God wants you to be. You can determine this by how the person interacts with you. Is she truly committed to helping you grow in your faith? Does that individual actively love you as you are but also show interest in helping you become better—reaching the full potential the Father created you to experience? Does she inspire you to trust that "nothing will be impossible with God" (Luke 1:37)?

3. *Delight you*—bringing you happiness and comfort and helping you enjoy life. Look at the fruit that is produced when you're around that person. Are you energized, and do situations seem better when he is present? Does that individual bring out the best in you and stimulate you to put your gifts to use? When you are hurting, does he console you and help you overcome the trials you are facing? Does that person cheer on your strengths, encourage you in your weaknesses, and spur your personality to shine for the glory of God?

Of course, not every relationship in your life is so Christ-centered or motivational, but the very closest ones—the ones that ultimately shape your path—should be. So I truly hope you have godly people in your life who drive, develop, and delight you in a manner that helps you grow closer to the Father. Such spiritual influences, friends, and mentors can be an incredible treasure—not because of anything they have or who they are as far as the world is concerned, but because they faithfully accompany and support you on the path to all God has for you.

After all, my friend, you and I were never called to go it alone in this walk of faith. Consider why God established the church in the first place. He did so in order for us to have an inherent support network as His children—to give us guidance and direction for our lives; to provide strength, protection, and help in times of suffering and sorrow; and, of course, so we can be His representatives to a lost and dying world. This is why Hebrews 10:24–25 admonishes, "Let us consider how to stimulate one another to love and do good deeds, not forsaking our own assembling together, as is the habit of some, but encouraging one another; and all the more as you see the day drawing near."

The truth of the matter is that, eventually, a lack of encouragement and support from fellow Christians always takes a toll on our spiritual lives and invariably leads us to feelings of alienation and isolation. Why? Because without other believers, we find it difficult to counteract the ungodly messages of the world and we become easy targets for the enemy. This is why it's so incredibly important for us to invest in godly relationships with Christ-like friends and mentors who inspire us, hold us accountable, and challenge us spiritually.

You and I were never called to go it alone in this walk of faith.

God has engineered it so that it is in relationship with other members of the Body of Christ that we discover and fulfill His will for our lives. And when you have godly, Spirit-filled people accepting you, cheering you on, loving you, building you up, and ministering to you as you serve them—well, that's when you're positioned perfectly to experience the fullness of the Father's grace, power, and plan. That's a taste of heaven that you don't want to miss. So, friend, walk with wise men and women and be wise (Pr. 13:20). Seek out godly mentors and Christ-centered influences. Don't settle for less. Because there is absolutely no telling all God wants to do in and through your life or how another believer could help you get there.

4

Unexpected Intervention

O Lord my God, when I in awesome wonder
Consider all the worlds Thy hands have made,
I see the stars, I hear the rolling thunder,
Thy power throughout the universe displayed:
Then sings my soul, my Savior God, to thee:
How great Thou art! How great Thou art!
—STUART K. HINE, 1885

"Faith takes God without any ifs."
—DWIGHT L. MOODY

There will be times in your life when you've done all you can—you've obeyed the Father, you've stayed close to Him through Bible study and prayer, and you've sought out godly influences. Even so, there may still be details of your life that require soul-stretching trust that God is willing and able to help you. And in those difficult times, you may also receive blessings that you never even knew to ask for, blessings that come from the Lord unexpectedly. These are the Father's divine appointments and surprise visits—circumstances that only He can engineer to take your life on the path that it's supposed to be on.

UNANTICIPATED PROVISION

For example, when I turned seventeen in September 1949, I couldn't see how I would be able to go to college because I simply couldn't afford it. As you know, I delivered newspapers and made only $16 a week. I also got a side job washing cars at a local service station, which helped, but it was still far from what I needed to pay for college tuition, books, room and board, and whatever other expenses might arise. This caused me some stress, because I was set to graduate from George Washington High School on June 9, 1950, and my time to apply to the university was getting short.

As you might expect, Mother always encouraged me to pray. We would kneel together and ask the Father to provide for me, claiming the promise of Philippians 4:19, "My God will supply all your needs according to His riches in glory in Christ Jesus." After we prayed, my mother would say, "Charles, if God has called you to preach, He will give you everything you require to accomplish what He's planned for you. I don't know how He will do it, but I am certain He will."

By that time, I had left the Pentecostal Holiness Church and had begun attending Moffett Memorial Baptist with my girlfriend, Barbara Ann. The pastor of the Pentecostal Holiness Church, F. A. Dail, had retired, and I was longing for a change. So I asked my mother if she approved, and she replied, "If you can live as holy a life in the Baptist church as in the Pentecostal Holiness church, then it's all right with me."

Of course, Baptists in Danville weren't known for being as

righteous as the Pentecostals, but I thought I would take my chances all the same. And at the time, Moffett Memorial Baptist was the place to be—all of my friends were there, and the church was full every Sunday. Undeniably, the main draw was the pastor, Reverend David Hammock, who was a very kind and godly man. Reverend Hammock was a tremendous soul winner and gifted Bible preacher. I learned a great deal from him. Certainly, God was powerfully at work in that congregation, and I knew in my heart that the Father was leading me to make it my new church home.

Moreover, my association with Moffett Memorial opened up some opportunities that I would not have experienced otherwise. For example, I went to a Baptist summer program at the Massanetta Springs Camp and Conference Center in Harrisonburg, Virginia, because I heard they had a public-speaking contest there. I looked out at that

"God will give you everything you require to accomplish what He's planned for you."

huge crowd—the biggest crowd I had ever seen to that point—as I spoke to them about prayer. Apparently, I did something right because I came in second place in the competition. And that was just the encouragement I needed and the spark that would set my passion for proclaiming God's Word ablaze.

Not too long after that, I was invited to preach my first sermon at my old home church. Of course, I accepted. It was on a Sunday night, and I preached on Genesis 3. The title was "Where Art Thou?" It was about when God went to find Adam and Eve in the Garden of Eden, but they were both in hiding because they had sinned by eating from the Tree of the Knowledge of Good and Evil. I had studied and prayed all week—committing the points to memory, just as my grandfather had done before me. Granddad never used an outline or a script; in fact, there were only four marks in his entire Bible. I wanted to be like him, so I decided to forgo notes. Instead, I asked God to speak through me as powerfully as He had my grandfather.

My mother saw that I was a little anxious to be preaching in front of so many people I knew, so she walked into my room and said, "Before you go to church tonight, I want to give you a verse that the Lord has laid on my heart for you." She then read me Joshua 1:7–9:

> *Only be strong and very courageous; be careful to do according to all the law which Moses My servant commanded you; do not turn from it to the right or to the left, so that you may have success wherever you go. This book of the law shall not depart from your mouth, but you shall meditate on it day and night, so that you may be careful to do according to all that is written in it; for then you will make your way prosperous, and then you will have success. Have I not commanded you? Be strong and courageous! Do not tremble or be dismayed, for the Lord your God is with you wherever you go.*

As always, Mother knew just what I needed. As I walked the three blocks to the church, I memorized that wonderful passage. It gave me strength and confidence every step of the way. Then, right before I crossed the street to go into the church building, I stood by the light pole, quoting that verse to myself, and saying, "All right, Lord, this is it. This is my first sermon, and it is all for You. I know You are with me. You helped Granddad with his sermons, and I believe You can work through mine."

As soon as I walked up to the pulpit, the message began to flow. God gave me the words to say in a manner that surprised and delighted me. I can't begin to express the absolute joy I felt knowing that the Holy Spirit was in control and the Father was speaking through me.

That experience increased my yearning to preach the gospel, which fueled my desire to go to college and be trained in the ministry. As I said, at seventeen, I had no idea how I would pay for my education. It was difficult to have so much passion for something and see absolutely no way to get to it. I am certain you know what I mean. Like my grandfather before me, I wondered why the Father would give me such a deep desire to preach and then put such obstacles in my path.

So I did what I knew to do—I returned to the promise of Joshua 1:7–9, meditating on the Word day and night, counting on the Father to give me everything I needed for success and trusting that He would be with me no matter what.

And true to form, God was right on time, as He always is.

The day is still crystal clear in my mind. It was evening and I was standing on the corner of North Main and Moffett Memorial Streets, talking to my good friend Julian Phillips about the difficulties I was facing in financing my education. I said, "Julian, I know God has called me. I don't have any doubt about that. And I really want to go to school, but I just don't see how I'll be able to afford it. I know God will work it out, but it all seems impossible right now."

True to form, God was right on time, as He always is.

Julian listened to me patiently, as any good friend would. But at just that moment, a man walked by who caught his attention. It was none other than Reverend Hammock.

Julian called out, "Mr. Hammock, Charles believes the Lord has called him to preach, but he doesn't have any money to go to school. He needs some help. Can you do anything for him?"

Reverend Hammock thought for a moment and then replied with

a smile, "I think I can help, Charles. Come see me and let's talk about it."

So a couple of days later, I made an appointment and went to his office, and I told him about my circumstances. About a month later, Reverend Hammock informed me, "Charles, I've worked it out for you to have a four-year scholarship to go to the University of Richmond. How does that sound?"

I was astounded. Just like that, the Father met my financial needs—not just for my first year of college, but for as long as it would take to get a degree in history. I hadn't even considered asking the pastor for assistance. But that is how the Lord engineers the details of our lives. We have no idea whom or what the Father will work through to get us where we need to be, but we can absolutely trust Him to get us there. What a good and mighty God we serve!

I left for college with only $75 to my name, and I graduated from the University of Richmond four years later, on June 7, 1954, debt free and with increased faith in God's awesome provision. Two years after that, on August 19, 1956, I was ordained into the ministry at Moffett Memorial Baptist. The Lord had done it all, orchestrating all the circumstances of my life in order to provide for all my needs.

UNFORESEEN PURPOSES

God will do that, friend. He will put people and opportunities in your path that you know could come only from Him. And when He does—when He arranges those unseen details to make the impossible possible for you—it is absolutely awesome. But be warned, He will also close doors that are important to you in order to grow your faith and lead you on His specific path for your life. And that's just as amazing.

For example, when I was in college, I joined the Air Force ROTC because of my profound respect for the military. I also signed up for the armed services for four years after I graduated, along with several of my friends. Of course, the Korean War was going on at that time. It began in 1950 and ended in 1953, which meant it was raging throughout most of my college career. So I understood that being sent to the front lines was a real possibility. In fact, when I first got to the University of Richmond, we all lived in the army barracks there because they did not have enough dorms for everyone. So the reality of it was all around me. It wasn't until a friend told me he wanted to give up his private dorm room—B-17 in Jeter Hall—that I got my own place where I could really get alone and seek the Lord in prayer.

My goal in the military was to be a chaplain to the brave, hard-working troops who were defending our nation. If anyone needed the encouragement of God's presence, they surely did. And I certainly had plenty of practice counseling people. I can't tell you how many times I opened the door of B-17 Jeter Hall to a hurting soul who simply wanted to talk about some difficult situation in his life—his girlfriend, finances, purpose in life, or whatever it might be. So I looked forward to ministering to soldiers—giving them comfort from Scripture and teaching them to cling to the Father through the thickest of battles.

But in that last year of college, I felt that the Lord was calling me to go to seminary before I did anything else in life. This change in direction was difficult for me, especially since I had made that four-year commitment to the ROTC. But the Father made it very clear: He wanted me to get a theological education, and each day the conviction became greater.

I prayed for a long time, made an appointment with the colonel on staff, and went down to the ROTC headquarters to meet with him. I figured if it were really the Lord's will that I go on to seminary, He would make a way. I recalled Granddad's words: "Charles, if God tells you to run your head through a brick wall, you head for the wall, and when you get there, God will make a hole for it." I lowered my head and prepared for impact.

The colonel was an imposing, serious man, outfitted in his full military uniform. I recall thinking how silly and unreasonable my request would sound to him. Only the Lord could stop him from saying, "Tough luck, son," and sending me on my way.

So I just told him, "Colonel, I've loved these three years in the ROTC, and I am so grateful for everything I have learned. But God is calling me to preach, and I really believe He wants me to go to seminary before I do anything else. Would you allow me to drop out so I can go?"

He looked at my enlistment papers. Then he looked at me. Without saying a word, in one swift motion, he tore up the papers. Not one more word of explanation was required on either part. The Lord had put that colonel in my path as an undeniable confirmation of His will for me. I was going to seminary.

Though I did not understand why the Father would not allow me to minister to our military then, I see now why He sent me to seminary first. I had a lot to learn. And throughout the years, He has blessed me with opportunities to serve our troops through the Armed Forces Radio and Television Service, which broadcasts on bases throughout the world. Also, in 2007, we developed the In Touch Messenger—a solar-powered audio device with specially chosen sermons to encourage and instruct the soldiers who serve so faithfully. I am very humbled and grateful that the Father has answered my prayers above and beyond imagination and has allowed me to be a kind of chaplain to so many men and women in uniform. If you or your loved ones are in the armed forces, please know how profoundly I appreciate your sacrifice for our nation and that you are in my prayers daily.

Although the Messenger continues as a ministry to our military, it has expanded to become a tool through which the gospel is proclaimed throughout the world. When we first developed the Messenger, we had no idea how God would use it—even reaching troops in other countries in ways we never anticipated.

The Lord had put that colonel in my path as an undeniable confirmation of His will for me. I was going to seminary.

For example, in 2014, pro-Russian groups tried to force Ukraine to join the Russian Federation. There was terrible conflict and unrest in Ukraine, as armies from both sides rose up to do combat. It was a tense and volatile situation. Understanding their need for the hope that only Jesus offers, one of In Touch Ministries' partners carried more than thirty-five hundred Messengers into the area—the majority of which were distributed to Ukrainian troops.

At one point, however, the Russians bombed the airport at Donetsk, where a group of Ukrainian soldiers were hiding. Sadly, the majority of the servicemen perished during that attack—but not before they heard the gospel. Every soldier had a Messenger in his pocket. My hope is that they were able to accept Jesus as their Savior and that each of them had the comfort and assurance of eternal life before he passed away.

But here is the truly miraculous thing that happened. Those

Russian soldiers went to the airport to survey the damage, found the Messengers, and became fascinated by them. One of the military commanders did an interview with journalists that was broadcast over two of the main Russian news channels, which Russian-speaking people all over the world can see. Of all the things he could have talked about, he said:

> *In the pockets of every soldier we found this device. It doesn't require any batteries. It is solar-powered. This is the way they are zombie-ing Ukrainian solders—assuring them hope. Encouraging them to wait for help to come. But even if help does not come, it's not going to be bad. They are not afraid to die because somewhere they are waiting for them with open arms. That's what I heard. But then, you know, I listened to it myself and I began to believe it myself, if I'm going to die like they did in that rubble nothing bad would happen to me.*

Of course, what this man was talking about is that the soldiers were falling under conviction of the Holy Spirit. They weren't becoming zombies—they were being saved! The gospel of Jesus Christ was setting them free!

In fact, we received a report that one of the Russian separatist soldiers went to a Christian church—fully armed and in uniform—and stood at the entrance, quietly watching the proceedings and enjoying the teaching of God's Word. Apparently, when the service concluded, the man asked the pastor if it would be all right for him to come again the following Sunday and attend the services. The pastor replied, "Yes, of course you are welcome here. But next time, please don't bring your gun."

The next Sunday, the Russian returned without his weapon,

clothed in civilian apparel. Pleasantly surprised that the man had left his military garb behind, the pastor greeted the soldier warmly and asked him what had happened. Why the complete change?

He replied, "I repented, so I returned my gun and my uniform because I don't need them anymore."

Isn't that absolutely amazing? To think that those Messengers traveled from Atlanta, Georgia, to our partner in Ukraine, to those Ukrainian soldiers, to finally end up in the hands of those Russian troops, so that they could believe the Good News of salvation through Jesus Christ. Only God could do that!

And that is just one story among the hundreds I receive. I am so exceedingly grateful for all the Father is doing and all the ways He is getting the gospel to the whole world. And it all came about because the Lord put it in my heart to serve the troops, and that call never went away.

UNIMAGINED ASSOCIATIONS

The point is that sometimes we simply don't know why certain things happen to us. We are confused and heartbroken, but we have to understand that God is doing something greater—engineering our circumstances in a manner that we do not understand but in a way that will benefit us immensely in the long run.

In the previous chapter I mentioned that my first great crisis in prayer came because of a girl I was dating, Barbara Ann Johnson. It was difficult to break up with her, but I knew it was the right thing to do. And later, when I met Anna, it was actually prayer that brought us together.

I was introduced to Anna Margaret Johnson at Grove Avenue

Baptist Church while I was in college. My friend Charlie Fuller had invited me to attend, and though the church was bigger than the others I was accustomed to, I found it to be a very welcoming place. In fact, the pastor, Byron Wilkinson, would eventually ask me to preach there.

I met Annie on a Sunday night. The chairman of the deacons approached me, put Annie's hand in mine, and said, "Charles, I want you to meet the girl you're going to marry." At the time, I thought he was being silly. She was a very nice young lady, of course, but she wasn't necessarily the type I usually went for. But Annie was pretty, very bright, artistic, and best of all, she had a deep passion for God— so she was certainly someone I wanted to know. It wasn't long before I thought that she was the most godly, purest, most committed, sold-out Christian gal I'd ever met.

As God would engineer it, Annie and I were both headed to the same destination—Southwestern Baptist Theological Seminary. In fact, when a friend and I needed a ride from Virginia to the school in Fort Worth, Texas, Annie was the one who took us in her car.

At that point in my life, most of my friends were married, so I didn't have anyone to pray with. I asked Annie if she would mind praying with me. She agreed. We would meet on campus, outside under the trees before dinner. Later, she and I found a room in the music building where we could pray. We sought God together about our personal needs, about our struggles with classes and the volume of material we were expected to learn, and about knowing and doing His will, especially after we finished seminary. The more time I spent with her, the more I realized how much I cherished her. I was not only drawn to her personality, I also admired her knowledge and faith. She always seemed to have a balanced and thorough knowledge of God's

Word and a very deep desire to serve the Lord. Her passion for Christ inspired me, and I could not imagine living without her.

One afternoon when we were together, I remember opening my eyes and looking at her lovely face as she spoke to our heavenly Father so beautifully and movingly in prayer. One thought kept flooding my mind: *God, I think I'm in love with this girl.* I was totally surprised, but so grateful to the Lord for knowing better than I did what I really wanted and needed.

"Charles," the deacon said, "I want you to meet the girl you're going to marry."

We had both grown up in difficult situations—Annie's parents were divorced—so neither of us was very open with our emotions at first. In fact, it took me some time to tell her how I felt about her. I wanted to make absolutely certain that I really meant it before I ever told her I loved her.

I planned how I would do it—looking deep into her eyes and saying, "I love you," with all my heart. Like any young person would, I imagined it was going to be an extraordinary experience to remember, where she would return my sentiments and all would be grand.

But when that moment came, all she said was, "Thank you."

No music. No fireworks. No miraculous moment.

That was it. "Thank you."

I thought, *Well, I wasn't expecting that!* Gratefully, it wasn't too long before she reciprocated and told me she loved me, too.

Naturally, I had to tell my mother about the lady the Father had led me to. So I wrote to her and told her all about Annie. I confessed that I wanted to marry her and that I believed she was the wife God had chosen for me. It was important to me that they meet, and I prayed that they would get along well. But it was about six months before I could arrange to take Annie to Danville so she could get to know my mom.

I will never forget the moment when the two loves of my life met for the first time. We drove up, and Mother ran to Annie's side of the car, hugging her and telling her how much she loved her as soon as the door was open. It didn't matter that Mother had never seen or talked to Annie before. My mom already felt a tight bond with Annie because she had been praying for her—my future wife—for almost as long as she'd prayed for me. And of course, Mom loved me with all of her heart, and anybody I loved, she would care for, too.

I couldn't have been happier. It was absolutely wonderful to have someone in my life who shared my commitment to Christ like Annie did—so we didn't wait long. We were married on August 6, 1955. I recall driving away from the wedding reception, the dust flying up behind the car like we were leaving the past behind. I had this awesome sense that we were starting fresh and new. The future seemed so bright and full of possibilities for us.

But that unencumbered feeling of freedom and joy didn't last long. The truth of the matter was, I didn't really know what to do next. As a newly married man, the desire to provide for my wife was second only to my longing to serve God. It occurred to me that graduation wasn't too far away, and I had no idea what the process was for getting a church. Likewise, I didn't have many connections to recommend me to a willing congregation.

You can imagine the thoughts that crossed my mind: Whom did I need to meet with? Where should I apply? Who could help me find a church? So with a year until graduation, I prayed that the Father would open a door.

We were living in a tiny apartment at 1107 Fairmont Drive in Fort Worth at the time. Each evening, I would go to my "prayer room"—a place in the back corner of the living room marked out with a blanket, where I could be alone with God. One night while I was down praying, the Lord spoke in a way that was so crystal clear it was as if He'd written it on my soul. He said, "Whatever you accomplish in life, you'll have to accomplish on your knees." Period. I wouldn't find a church or a ministry to serve in because of my talent, education, eloquence, connections, or anything else. If I wanted to accomplish things that had eternal value, I would have to depend on God for all of it—and I would have to do so in prayer. It was another pivotal moment in my spiritual journey that would shape me for the rest of my life. I continued to seek the Father and kept my eyes open for His activity.

At the time, the only option that seemed even remotely available to us was the mission field. So Annie and I went to the Missions Conferences at Southwestern Seminary and listened to the faithful men and women who were serving the Lord in remote places and seeing His awesome power and provision at work. What inspiring and convicting testimonies! At these conferences, I would stand there and pray, "Oh God, I'm willing to go. But if You're going to call me into the mission field, please call Annie, too."

> *"Whatever you accomplish in life, you'll have to accomplish on your knees."*

She was asking the same thing: "Father, I'll do whatever You want me to do. But if You lead me to go into missions, please call Charles, too."

So at the end of our second year at seminary, in the spring of 1956, Annie and I decided to see where the Lord was leading by applying to the Home Missions Board of the Southern Baptist Convention (now called the North American Mission Board) for the summer. They offered us an opportunity to volunteer at a small church in Fresno, California, where Annie could sing and I could preach.

Annie and I talked about it, and we thought it might be a good thing to go. After all, if the church liked us, perhaps they would invite us back full-time after seminary. Yet neither of us had peace about it. Moreover, one Saturday morning, I was praying about the summer and felt a terrible burden. I could not shake it. I told Annie, "I just need to spend time talking to the Lord about this."

I prayed all day long, as did she. Finally, God spoke to my heart, "Charles, California is *your* plan. It sounds good, it looks good, and it's a great plan. But it is not My will for your life. You must lay it down."

Annie and I were certainly willing to obey Him and forget the opportunity in Fresno, but we found ourselves without anything to do for the summer. Annie's family owned a cottage up on Lake Lure in Hickory Nut Gorge, North Carolina, and her father suggested we stay there. The prospect of resting for three months after four years of college and two years of seminary seemed very inviting but not very spiritual. I struggled with the idea that the Lord would send us to a big, beautiful lake up in the mountains to enjoy ourselves instead of the mission field to preach the gospel. That couldn't possibly be the will of God, could it? But whenever I prayed, that seemed to be where He was leading.

So Annie and I went to Lake Lure and enjoyed the rest. And boy, am I glad we did!

One day in August 1956, the last month we were staying at Lake Lure, we went fishing, hoping to catch some bluegill that we could enjoy for dinner. All of a sudden, we heard someone calling for us from the dock, so we rowed a little closer so we could hear him.

He shouted, "Is your name Charles Stanley?"

"Yes, sir," I hollered back as we continued to paddle.

"Are you a seminary student?"

"Yes, sir."

"I'm a deacon from the Fruitland Baptist Church, and I need to talk to you."

When we finally got to the dock, he explained that his pastor, Reverend Noah Abraham Melton, was going to be on vacation for two weeks and they needed someone to preach. He asked me if I would be willing to fill the pulpit that next Sunday.

I agreed. I hadn't preached that much and felt somewhat inadequate, but I felt compelled to accept his invitation.

So that Sunday, I preached at Fruitland Baptist Church near Hendersonville, North Carolina. They asked me to come back the following week and I agreed, glad to know that they sensed God's wisdom and presence in what I'd said.

To my surprise, that next Sunday, Reverend Melton was present for the services and listened intently as I spoke.

After the evening meeting that same day, the congregation had a reception, and they invited Annie and me to attend. At one point during the party, the pastor and a group of men pulled me aside to talk. It was then that Reverend Melton—a truly great saint of God— told me that he had been at Fruitland for forty-seven years, and now the Lord was moving him to retire. He had met with the other leaders of the church, and they felt that God was leading them to call me as their pastor.

That caught me completely by surprise. I said, "But I've still got a year of seminary left."

Reverend Melton replied, "We're happy to wait for you, Charles, because we believe you're just what we need." He continued, "In fact, we're going to build you a new house. We planned to construct one for the next pastor, anyway. So you go on back to school. We'll have a brand-new house built for you by the time you're done."

I told them I would have to pray about it, which they understood. About two weeks later, Annie and I returned to seminary, and I continued to pray about the opportunity for the next three months. I wanted to be absolutely certain it was God's will.

Naturally, the people from Fruitland kept in touch. In December 1956, I received a letter from them saying that the members had voted unanimously to make me their pastor. They were convinced I was the man to lead their church.

Likewise, in April 1957, a month before I graduated seminary, I received an unexpected letter from the president of the Fruitland Baptist Bible Institute, Dr. J. C. Canipe. The school was just across the street from Fruitland Baptist Church, and Reverend Melton had taught several subjects there. Since Reverend Melton was retiring, Dr. Canipe wondered if I would be willing to teach some classes to pastors who did not have an opportunity to attend seminary. Again, I committed myself to prayer.

Throughout that time, however, I was absolutely astounded to think of the opportunities before me. Just a year earlier, I had been so disheartened, wondering how I would find a church and seeing no options in view. But God had orchestrated everything in a way I could never have imagined—and had begun doing so many years before I even knew to worry about where I would serve. I thought about how Annie's family had purchased the property at Lake Lure—which was less than thirty miles from Fruitland Baptist—before Annie and I had even met. How God allowed me to meet Annie in Virginia and how He'd moved us to Southwestern Seminary at the same time before we even knew we would be together. How the Lord had stopped us from going to Fresno, and how simultaneously He was moving in Reverend Melton's heart to retire. I could go on and on about all of the details that it took for Him to get me from point A in Fort Worth to point B in Hendersonville—and probably never figure out even a tenth of them. I don't even know how that deacon knew to look for me at Lake Lure that summer.

God had orchestrated everything in a way I could never have imagined—and had begun doing so many years before I even knew to worry about where I would serve.

But the point is that God will move heaven and earth to show us His will and then He will provide everything necessary for us to do it. There is no doubt about that.

GOD'S UNEXPECTED INTERVENTION FOR YOU

So be encouraged. There may be many times in your life when the road ahead appears dark or impossible, and you feel absolutely helpless to do anything about it. In fact, you may be facing one of those seasons right now.

Perhaps there is something you require to live or move forward— like when I needed tuition for college. You do everything you can, but it is not enough and you simply do not see how the Lord could possibly provide for you.

Maybe you're experiencing a closed door to a deep desire of your heart—such as when God called me to go to seminary instead of being a military chaplain. You don't understand why the Father would lead you away from something that means so much to you and seems to be a wonderful way to fulfill His purpose for you.

It could even be that your future lies in the balance—as mine did in seminary. There are no open doors, no possibilities, and you have no idea about how to proceed. You are seeking God's direction, but He does not seem to answer your cries. So you continue to wait and to pray.

Does any of this sound familiar? Friend, if your prayers seem unanswered, your needs unmet, or the road ahead completely blocked, don't lose hope. Instead, trust that God never rejects a person who is seeking Him. And He doesn't leave a believing soul in such a state unless He is about to do something astounding. As Lamentations 2:25–26 reminds us, "The LORD is good to those who wait for Him, to the person who seeks Him. It is good that he waits silently for the salvation of the LORD."

We see this all through Scripture. Consider when Jesus' friends Mary and Martha sent word that their brother Lazarus was deathly ill. John 11:4 teaches, "When Jesus heard this, He said, 'This sickness is not to end in death, but for the glory of God, so that the Son of God may be glorified by it.'" Then He waited two days before He went to see them (John 11:6).

I'm sure it didn't look like the Lord was getting any glory to Mary and Martha—just as our trials don't usually appear to magnify Him to us. In fact, we may view the painful things that happen to us—especially the delays—as the Lord's anger or rejection. But John 11:5 affirms that "Jesus loved Martha and her sister and Lazarus," so we are assured that He felt tenderness and affection for them. So it wasn't because He didn't care about them that He waited the two days—it was actually because He *did*! He expressed His love for them by delaying His arrival because He knew it would be more beneficial for them to see the mighty power of God at work than to spare them their momentary distress.

And so Mary and Martha had to experience the doubly painful bereavement of losing not only their beloved brother but also their one earthly provider. In fact, by the time Jesus got there, Lazarus had been in the grave four days.

But by waiting, they saw what very few people have ever seen— they saw Lazarus raised from the dead. They saw a preview of Jesus' power over the grave! They witnessed Christ's words proved true: "I am the resurrection and the life; he who believes in Me will live even if he dies, and everyone who lives and believes in Me will never die" (John 11:25).

Thankfully, the same is true for every person who knows Christ as his or her Lord and Savior: If God allows some difficulty or hardship in our lives, it is because He can bring forth some good purpose from it where we will know Him better, see His power, be cleansed from sin, or reflect His character more (Rom. 8:28).

So don't be discouraged or imagine that the trials and delays you are experiencing are because of the Father's disdain for you. Isaiah 30:18 explains, "The LORD longs to be gracious to you, and therefore He waits on high to have compassion on you. For the LORD is a God of justice; how blessed are all those who long for Him." It may seem that the Father is stripping away your last cords of earthly hope, but in truth He is working through your trials to stretch your faith, strengthen your trust in Him, and build your

> *By waiting, they saw a preview of Jesus' power over the grave!*

character. As with Mary and Martha, it is far more beneficial for you to see His perfectly unlimited power at work than to spare you from those seasons of adversity.

So when there appear to be no open doors and you have no idea about how to go on, trust God, open Scripture, and start reading. What the Father showed me is true for you as well—whatever you achieve in life, you'll have to accomplish on your knees in prayer. So the key is for you to listen to Him. Receive His guidance by taking note of the passages He brings to your attention. Watch how He works through your circumstances—through both the opportunities and the obstacles He allows on your path. Seek out godly counsel that is based on God's Word. And always be patient. If the Father doesn't answer you immediately, that just means you don't need to know yet.

> *If the Father doesn't answer you immediately, that just means you don't need to know yet.*

The point is to keep focusing on Jesus until you receive clear direction. He will speak to you through everything that happens to you if you're willing to listen. And the best part is that when you submit to God in this manner, He will provide for you, show you His faithfulness, and empower you by His Holy Spirit in ways you could never have envisioned or imagined.

5

Fields of Service

Be Thou my Vision, O Lord of my heart;
Naught be all else to me, save that Thou art.
Thou my best Thought, by day or by night,
Waking or sleeping, Thy presence my light.
—DALLAN FORGAILL, EIGHTH CENTURY

"Depend on it. God's work done in God's way will never lack
God's supply. He is too wise a God to frustrate His purposes
for lack of funds, and He can just as easily supply them ahead
of time as afterwards, and He much prefers doing so."
—JAMES HUDSON TAYLOR

Ministry is never what you imagine it to be. No matter how diligently
you study, how devotedly you seek God, or how faithfully you serve,
there will always be surprises—some good and some that are not so
pleasant. This is true first because ministry is based on our utter dependence on the Lord, and that means He will allow situations to arise
that stretch our faith in Him and our love for others. Second, ministry
is usually more difficult than we imagine because we're dealing with
people who are unpredictable and whose needs are overwhelming.

Third, we all have our own struggles, fears, and failures that will affect how we serve the Father. And finally, as believers we all have an enemy who is constantly trying to derail us, especially when we are making strides for the kingdom of God.

This is why you must set your mind and heart to serve Jesus and keep your focus on Him. As Colossians 3:23–24 says, "Whatever you do, do your work heartily, as for the LORD rather than for men, knowing that from the LORD you will receive the reward of the inheritance. It is the Lord Christ whom you serve." If you can remember Who it is that you are really serving, you can do your absolute best no matter the task or the mission field. And remember, the Lord first establishes your faithfulness in the small assignments before He offers you the big ones (Luke 19:11–26).

This is a lesson I learned early on. While I was in college, in between semesters, I worked in the bleachery division of Dan River Textile Mill for extra money. It was sweltering hot in there—usually over a hundred degrees—so it took only about twenty minutes of labor for me to be soaking wet with perspiration. It was a terrible place, and I did not like it one bit.

The Lord first establishes your faithfulness in the small assignments before He offers you the big ones.

But I needed that income and quickly realized that in order to survive at the mill, I would have to change my attitude about it. So I prayed, "Lord, I am going to do my job as if You are the boss. I am going to do this work to the absolute best of my ability because I want to honor You, and I want others to see You through me."

Likewise, while I was in seminary I got a job at a grocery store cleaning up. I had to scrub the tables and sweep up some awful messes. The first week I was there, I thought, *God, I'm in seminary learning how to serve You. I deserve better than this.* But I quickly realized that the mind-set I was expressing was the one He had set out to change in me.

After all, the Lord had called me to be a servant—*His* servant—and He had a right to put me wherever He wanted to. I thought of the apostle Paul in prison and how he had the wisdom and foresight to say, "My circumstances have turned out for the greater progress of the gospel, so that my imprisonment in the cause of Christ has become well known throughout the whole praetorian guard and to everyone else, and that most of the brethren, trusting in the LORD because of my imprisonment, have far more courage to speak the word of God without fear" (Phil. 1:12–14).

Like Paul, my job was to glorify God regardless of where He put me, fully trusting that my obedience would further the gospel in ways greater than any of my plans could. Of course, this is the task of each and every believer. You and I are called to love and serve the Lord to the best of our ability, with all our heart, mind, soul, and strength in *every* situation—no matter where we are. And more often than not, He will put us in situations that will stretch our capacity to grow us and glorify Himself.

Throughout my ministry, I've tried to keep my heart clear and open to God's calling, and He's led me to move several times. I can look back over those years now and easily see how wise the Lord's leading has been—even through the most difficult moves. During my time with each church, I've gotten to know many wonderful people, and I have learned invaluable lessons. I now recognize how each one was necessary in order to take the next step in obedience to Him.

EAGLE OR OYSTER?

As I said in the previous chapter, I began my formal ministry at Fruitland Baptist Church, a small congregation in the mountains of Hendersonville, North Carolina, in June 1957. They were a fine group of people—salt-of-the-earth mountain folks—and I was motivated to serve them wholeheartedly. So was Annie. We wanted to reach everyone in the community, so she drew a map of the area, including all the houses. We worked diligently to determine the spiritual condition of every household by visiting each family and sharing the gospel with any who had not accepted Christ. We put pins in the map to track our progress.

What struck me almost immediately, however, was that as fine as these people were, they lacked passion for the truth of God's Word and how it could shape their lives. And the things the people *would* get excited about—well, they were less than honoring to God. For example, they were very enthusiastic about the stills they had hidden up in the highlands, so bootlegging was a big problem. Likewise, a number of families were embroiled in terrible conflicts, which certainly hindered fellowship in the church.

All this seemed so wrong to me—I wanted better than that for Fruitland. I trusted the truth of Psalm 103:19, "The LORD has established His throne in the heavens, and His sovereignty rules over all." God—the Creator of all things—could certainly change their hearts through the indwelling Holy Spirit. But that would require a willing servant to proclaim the difficult truth to them and explain the importance of obedience. I prayed that I was up to the task.

While I was in seminary, I'd heard such a man of God preach. His name was Wallie Amos (W. A.) Criswell, and a friend had given me an old-fashioned wire recording of one of his sermons. Dr. Criswell—who had been pastor of the First Baptist Church of Dallas since October 1944—was based about forty miles from Southwestern Seminary, which I was attending. So on September 12, 1954, Annie and I decided to go hear him preach in person.

God—the Creator of all things—could certainly change their hearts through the indwelling Holy Spirit.

It was astounding. I had never been in a church as big as First Baptist Dallas in my life—so many people assembling together to worship the true and living God. I was inspired by the awe and possibility of such a body serving Christ in this lost and dying world. But even more striking was Dr. Criswell himself. When he stood up at the pulpit, a hush fell over the congregation. He opened his Bible to Romans 5:1–2 and began to preach a sermon titled "This Grace Wherein We Stand" with authority and conviction that could come only from the Holy Spirit. He had an incredible grasp of Scripture and how it related to ancient history as well as to current world events.

Dr. Criswell used an illustration in that sermon that stuck with me:

> *Against the day of the personal intervention of Almighty God, there are two ways that we can do. One: We can live in an escapist world of defeat and despair: give it up, give it up—no heart to try, no strength or will to resist . . . Or, we can rise to meet the storm. We, by God's grace, can try to measure up in this awful and awesome day and hour.*
>
> *Could I liken it facetiously to an oyster and an eagle? You know, that little oyster is an unusual little creation. God gave him a wonderful house in which to live. All he has to do is to open his house,*

and take in his food, and close his house and shut out his enemies; and
there he is so perfectly secure in his escapist world on the inside of his
little shell—right there he is. But I don't know of any fish more easily
caught and crushed and cooked than an oyster. If I could facetiously
remark about him: He always ends up in the soup.

The eagle is an unusual creation of Almighty God . . . When the
hurricane comes and the fierce storms blow, the eagle sets his pinions
against the blow and he rises with it, and up and up is he carried
until finally he soars in God's blue sky above the hurricane and the
storm. We can live like an oyster in our little house—in an escapist's
world—or we can rise to meet the storm.[2]

Dr. Criswell inspired me profoundly. First, I wanted to preach
from Scripture with enthusiasm and authority as he did. He did not
rely on showmanship and rhetorical strategies, as some pastors do.
Rather, he relied on his relationship with Christ. Thankfully, on this
topic Dr. Criswell and my grandfather taught me a great deal: They
both trusted in the truth of God that's found in the Word of God
that's communicated and empowered through the Spirit of God. That
was the supernatural power in their preaching that reaches down into
our very spirit and moves us to genuine change—something that no
human communication technique can reproduce.

And second, I did not intend to be an escapist with my life, simply
managing the dark chaotic storms and hoping they wouldn't catch up
to me, as many often do. It is a choice every minister of the gospel and
every child of God must make. Will we be oysters or eagles? Will we
shut our eyes to the problems, playing along to get along? Or will we
be a light to the world, trusting that God will work through us to lead
people out of the darkness (Matt. 5:14–16)?

I wanted to confront whatever tempest might arise, trusting that "those who wait for the LORD will gain new strength; they will mount up with wings like eagles, they will run and not get tired, they will walk and not become weary" (Isa. 40:31). And so for Fruitland, I didn't want to merely cope with the problems that were present; my aim was to uproot them. My goal wasn't for people at church to just sit back, listen to my sermons, and think, *Wasn't that wonderful?* I prayed that God would transform them by renewing their minds, so that they could obey the good, acceptable, and perfect will of the Father (Rom. 12:2). I prayed that the Holy Spirit would give them a con-

> *I didn't want to merely cope with the problems that were present; my aim was to uproot them.*

viction to grow up, be like Christ, and serve the Lord out of genuine love and commitment. So in my Bible, I wrote out these guidelines for every message I would preach:

1. Speak out of a <u>clear conscience</u>.
2. Speak <u>words of Scripture</u>.
3. Speak to a <u>person's conscience</u>.
4. Speak from your <u>own experience</u>.
5. Speak with <u>clear, factual words of truth</u>.
6. Speak with <u>grace, love, and joy</u>.
7. Speak under the <u>Holy Spirit's guidance</u>.

I then poured my heart into proclaiming God's Word. I studied and prayed over every sermon as if it were the only one I would ever preach.

PROCLAIMING GOD'S WORD

Early on in my ministry, I learned a twofold process for developing messages, and I have followed it consistently throughout the years.

I FIRST MAKE SURE MY RELATIONSHIP WITH GOD IS RIGHT. If my personal, intimate relationship with the Lord isn't right, then nothing else will be. After all, a man can preach only as well as he prays.

Scripture reminds us of this. As Peter and John testified before the rulers and scribes, their message had power—not because of their credentials or great communication techniques, but because of their profound relationship with Christ. Acts 4:13 testifies that when those priests and elders "observed the confidence of Peter and John and understood that they were uneducated and untrained men, they were amazed and began to recognize them as having been with Jesus." The very power of God flows in and through us as we spend time with Him.

So, in my times of prayer and studying His Word, I try to stay disciplined and seek to have:

- *A clean heart.* I make sure that I've confessed and sincerely repented of every sin and failure that I am aware of so that my communication with the Father will be unhindered.
- *A clear mind.* I trust God to give me a clear mind so I won't be preoccupied with external matters or a wrong view. I also seek to have His perspective on Scripture and what is going on in people's lives.
- *A balanced schedule and healthy life.* I ask Him to reveal if there is anything unbalanced about my schedule or unhealthy about

my life, because either of those things can distract us from preaching the Word in a manner that best represents Him. A balanced schedule and healthy life are crucial to our serving God well.

- *Godly relationships.* I pray for godly relationships to keep me accountable and help me carry out the goals God calls us to achieve together.
- *Courageous obedience.* I want to be courageous enough to be obedient to God—regardless of what He might require—before I even begin to plan what I will say in the sermon.

When those aspects of my relationship with the Father are right, I know I can accomplish whatever He calls me to do.

THE SECOND THING I DO AS I DEVELOP THE MESSAGE IS TO ASK GOD'S DIRECTION. The following are principles I learned at Southwestern Baptist Theological Seminary under my favorite preaching professor, H. C. Brown. When I walked into his class for the first time, I had preached very few sermons, so I was excited and open to his instruction. He laid a strong foundation for my sermon preparation and delivery. I shall forever be grateful for all he taught me. This is my general process:

1. *I ask God what His goal is for the sermon.* Every message is an opportunity for the Lord to impact people's lives. So what is it He wants to do in and through them? How does He want them to be transformed into the image of Christ? You cannot think about yourself, what you want, or how you feel and expect to influence other people's lives. You have to trust the Lord to show you what needs to be addressed.

2. *I recognize His leading through the burden He places on my heart.* The Lord generally pinpoints some aspect of the Christian life or a need that should be confronted by helping me understand the heaviness of it. And once He does, I usually cannot wait to preach about it. He allows me to feel the weight and urgency of the message, and He undergirds it with the energy and desire to help people walk in a manner that honors Him.

3. *I then ask God to lead me to the passage of Scripture that would best help the people to walk in obedience to Him.* Once He identifies the verses, I ask Him, "What does this passage of Scripture say? How can I explain it to Your people in a way that will either meet their need or help them walk in the plans You have for them?"

4. *From there, I gather support materials.* I ask the Lord to show me everything that is needed for His goals to be accomplished in the message. To this day, I take a legal pad and a pen, write the theme of the message at the top of a fresh page, and begin writing down everything God calls to mind and every point of research I encounter. I then number every statement.

5. *Next comes what I call "the mystery moment."* I look at all the information and ask the Lord, "How do I put this all together in the way that would best bring You glory and motivate Your people?" And I listen for the Father to show me how to clearly and effectively organize all of those points and biblical principles so that the people can walk away with one thought that will drive them to faith and obedience. Once He shows me what He wants me to say, the outline just flows. I don't ever write the sermon out. I just write the points in my Bible and let Him lead.

6. *Then I go to sleep and let God sink the truth deep into my sub-conscious.* There is something supernatural that happens in our spirits when you and I slumber. The Lord continues to speak to us and etches His truth on our minds. So I always keep my sermon notes next to me as I sleep, in case there is anything more the Father wants me to say or a clearer way He wants me to communicate His message.

7. *Finally, I trust the Holy Spirit to plant the principles of Scripture in people's hearts and help them walk worthy of the Savior.* The Holy Spirit is the One who really motivates and transforms those I speak to. He is the One who inspires the words as I say them, and He is the One who makes the message poignant and life changing for those who hear. It's a supernatural exchange that takes place. As the apostle Paul said, "My message and my preaching were not in persuasive words of wisdom, but in demonstration of the Spirit and of power" (1 Cor. 2:4). There is just no other way to preach the gospel than in the power and direction of the Holy Spirit.

So from the beginning of my ministry at Fruitland, that's what I did. I did not hold back and did everything as the Lord led. Of course, this did not happen without a price. I experienced a terrible spiritual attack. You see, the enemy hates it when you and I commit ourselves to being obedient and faithful to God, and he knows right where to strike us to discourage us.

Fruitland Baptist Church had only a handful of members in those days, and during the freezing North Carolina winters, even fewer people showed up to the services. So when I looked out from the pulpit and saw all the empty pews, the enemy would whisper, "Look at that.

All of your preparation and nobody's here. What a complete waste of time. No one wants to hear you preach. What did you expect? You have no business meddling in their lives. They'll probably all end up leaving."

I knew those ungodly, disheartening thoughts weren't from the Father, so I would pray, and He always comforted me, "Charles, do your best every Sunday. Study the Word, pray, and seek Me for every sermon you preach. I have a plan for you that is beyond what you can imagine, but to get there, you have to be faithful here. Just trust Me and see what happens."

So that's what I did. I claimed the promise of Psalm 138:8 (TLB): "The LORD will work out His plans for my life." And I can gratefully say that none of that preparation was in vain. In fact, the Lord has done vastly more on my behalf than I have ever dreamed. Likewise, throughout my life I have seen it proved true again and again—it is always worthwhile to trust God and do as He says, even when it means flying straight into the storm.

The same is true for you. The enemy knows how to discourage you. The message may be different, but the effect is the same: He makes you feel futile, unwanted, and without hope. But don't believe him. The Lord God Almighty is the One who helps you, and He will not fail you. And He has given you the storms you experience for a purpose—to transform you and those around you. So obey Him, turn in to the tempest, and don't be afraid. There is absolutely no telling what He will do through your life as you obey Him. Allow what the prophet Isaiah has written to be your strength and

> *It is always worthwhile to trust God and do as He says, even when it means flying straight into the storm.*

your song: "The Lord God helps Me, therefore, I am not disgraced; therefore, I have set My face like flint, and I know that I will not be ashamed. He who vindicates Me is near . . . Who is among you that fears the LORD, that obeys the voice of His servant, that walks in darkness and has no light? Let him trust in the name of the LORD and rely on his God" (Isa. 50:7–8, 10).

EMPOWERED, EQUIPPED, AND ABLE

As I said in the previous chapter, in addition to the call I received from the church, I got a letter from the president of the Fruitland Baptist Bible Institute (FBBI), Dr. J. C. Canipe. Since Reverend Melton was retiring, Dr. Canipe asked me to consider teaching homiletics, preaching, and evangelism in the institute.

This was an astounding request to me, considering I was still in seminary when it was made. I felt incredibly out of my depth. Most of the 160 students enrolled at FBBI were older than I was—ordained pastors with years of experience in their churches. They simply hadn't been given the opportunity to attend seminary as I had. But I prayed about it for a long time because I felt so profoundly inadequate for the task. Yet over and over again, the Father confirmed that it was His will for me.

Finally I prayed, "Lord, I don't understand all of this, and it's not anything I sought out for myself. You're the One who brought me this opportunity, and I know You are in this. I believe You are moving me to accept this assignment, so I'm just going to trust You in it."

The confidence that God could do in and through me far more than my natural gifts and abilities could possibly achieve was due in part to a book I read in seminary: *The Holy Spirit: Who He Is and What He Does* by R. A. Torrey. Torrey was a pastor who preached alongside the revivalist Dwight L. Moody on his evangelistic crusades and who would eventually become the superintendent of the Moody Bible Institute. Certainly, he was a great man of God by any measure. But in his book, Torrey admitted that he—like me—didn't feel adequate to the tasks the Father had for him.

In fact, Torrey described his early ministry as absolute torture because he was so painfully bashful and so fearful of failing. He had an awful time even speaking with others on a personal level, so public speaking was unbearably frightening to him. He couldn't even recite scripted speeches in front of his own mother and father! The task of preaching the gospel appeared to be completely out of the realm of possibility. He wrote, "If there was ever a man who by natural temperament was utterly unfit to preach, it was me."[3] But Torrey understood that this was what God was calling him to do, so he obeyed, regardless of the intense discomfort it caused him.

Unfortunately, the fear did not end for Torrey after completing seminary or even when he became a pastor. Torrey explained that the unease was continuous in those first years. He would feel some relief after finishing his messages on Sunday. "But then," he wrote, "the dreadful thought would take possession of me, 'Well, you've got to begin tomorrow morning to get ready for next Sunday.' "[4] And the overwhelming anxiety would begin again.

As you can imagine, I was riveted by Torrey's story. If a man whom God had used so powerfully had such failings and doubts, there was certainly hope for me. I didn't have enough money to buy the book, so I'd go to the bookstore, read a few pages, and put the book back on the shelf. Whenever I found a spare moment, I rushed back to the seminary bookstore to find out how God had transformed

FIELDS OF SERVICE *105*

Torrey's life so radically. And as I read, I came to understand how the
Father wanted to work though me.

You see, Torrey explained that "the Holy Spirit is not merely a
divine power that we get hold of and
use according to our will, but . . .
the Holy Spirit is a divine person
who gets hold of us and uses us according to His will."[5] So when He
calls us, we don't have to be afraid,
because He will actively instruct and
empower us to do all He's planned in advance for us to accomplish.
Torrey wrote,

> *Torrey explained that "the Holy Spirit is a divine person who gets hold of us and uses us according to His will."*

> *It is our privilege today to have the Holy Spirit, a living person,
> as our teacher. Every time we study our Bible it is possible for us to
> have this divine person, the author of the book, to interpret it for us,
> and to teach us its real and its innermost meaning. It is a precious
> thought. How many of us have often thought when we heard some
> great human teacher whom God has especially blessed to us, "If
> I could only hear that person every day, then I might make some
> progress in my Christian life." But listen, we can have a teacher
> more competent by far than the greatest human teacher that ever
> spoke on earth for our teacher every day, and that peerless teacher is
> the Holy Spirit.*[6]

Likewise, Torrey found that the Holy Spirit is "a helper always
at hand with his counsel and his strength and any form of help that
is needed."[7] In other words, the complete responsibility for our
task of serving the Lord belongs to God Himself, and He gives us
Himself through the Person of the Holy Spirit so the assignment can

be accomplished. That understanding frees us to accept all that the Father calls us to do with joy and confidence. As Torrey testified,

> *A glad day came, a day when . . . I stood up to preach, that though people saw me, there was another whom they did not see, but who stood by my side, and that all the responsibility was upon Him and all I had to do was get just as far back out of sight as possible and let Him do the preaching. From that day to this, preaching has been the joy of my life; I would rather preach than eat. Sometimes when I rise to preach, before I have uttered a word, the thought of Him standing beside me, able and willing to take charge of the whole meeting and do whatever needs to be done, has so filled my heart with exultant joy that I can scarcely refrain from shouting.*[8]

I was grateful for Torrey's candor. He showed that the weight of preaching God's Word and teaching others His ways is *supposed to be* too great for any man's shoulders. Only the Lord Almighty Himself should be entrusted with that profound duty, because only He searches people's hearts and knows what they really need.

Was I qualified to instruct those pastors on my own? No. But they could have no better Teacher than God Himself. So I submitted myself to the Lord as R. A. Torrey had done before me, trusting that the Father would take responsibility for my preaching if I would get out of His way.

I agreed to start teaching at FBBI in September 1957. I prayed and studied all summer, intent on doing my very best. But on the Friday before classes were to begin, I had a terrible restlessness in my soul. I realized I wasn't really ready for what awaited me on Monday morning. Although I was sealed with the Holy Spirit and He had indwelt me from the moment I'd accepted Christ as my Savior, I was not convinced that I was allowing Him full reign of my life, which I knew was needed.

So around four o'clock on that Friday afternoon, I knelt in prayer on the rug in my study, and I said to the Lord, "Father, You know I've been asking for Your help all summer long. I can't face those classes without Your Holy Spirit directing, equipping, and empowering me. God, I've done everything I know to do to give myself to You fully. I've prayed, I've fasted, and I've cried out to You. The only thing left for me to do is to claim what You've said in 1 John 5:14–15: 'This is the confidence that we have in Him, that if we ask anything according to His will, He hears us. And if we know that He hears us, whatever we ask, we know that we have the petitions that we have asked of Him.' So I am going to thank You, Father. I know that it is Your will that Your Holy Spirit be in full control of my life, so I know You've heard me and granted my request."

I submitted myself to the Lord, trusting that the Father would take responsibility for my preaching if I would get out of His way.

God's peace and freedom washed over me, and I knew He had filled me to overflowing with His Holy Spirit. On Monday, I walked into my first class with confidence, knowing that the Lord was guiding my every word and step. Thankfully, those pastors accepted me instantly, encouraged me immeasurably, and showed an incredible eagerness to learn. Only God could have done that. And I was so very grateful that He would bless me so powerfully.

Likewise, you may have an opportunity before you that is far beyond your gifts, talents, time, or reach. Yet you know for certain that God is calling you to step out in faith and take it on. Do it, friend, and do not be afraid. The task is supposed to be bigger than you are so that you will rely upon God and allow His Holy Spirit to work.

Simply give yourself over to Him completely, and you'll be amazed at all He does through you.

READY TO STAY—WILLING TO GO

Annie and I stayed at Fruitland for two years. In spite of the challenges we faced during our time there, the good far outweighed the bad—and we loved it. It was a place of firsts for us—our first ministry assignment, our first house together, and less than a year after we got there, our first child, Charles Andrew "Andy" Stanley, was born on May 16, 1958. It was a season full of praying, studying, preaching, and teaching. I'm still not quite sure how I got it all done—except that somehow the Father gave me the wisdom and energy to manage my tremendous workload. And whenever we needed a retreat, Annie and I would head to the mountains to hunt or to the lake for fishing.

That first field of service was a very spiritually productive season for us. God used that church and those circumstances to teach me many valuable lessons. For example, at one of Fruitland's Bible Conferences, I was preaching a sermon titled "The Will of God." When I finished, it was time for the main speaker to give his message. However, instead of doing so, he approached the platform and stated, "There is a time to preach and a time to pray. After that message, it's time to pray." As if on cue, we all got on our knees and had the most extraordinary and memorable prayer meeting. It was awesome, and we all rejoiced in the presence and power of God as we bowed before Him in adoration and worship.

Later that day, I would learn the real might behind the message I'd preached. At lunch, one of the ladies at our table told me, "Reverend

Stanley, this morning God told me to get into the closet in our room and pray for you while you preached." It was an unforgettable lesson, and God spoke straight to my heart through it: Prayer is what makes a message powerful and life changing—and not just my supplication *before* the sermon but also all the entreaties that occur *during* it. This is why I have prayer-warriors interceding for me while I preach to this day.

But as much as we loved being at Fruitland, I recall not feeling as if it was a permanent assignment. In fact, we hadn't been there a week when I said to Annie, "This is wonderful. But let's not sink our roots down too deep because the Lord may move us." It was such an odd thing for me to say, because at that point I had no reason to think we would ever leave Fruitland. As I said, we were in a brand-new house that the congregation had built for us. That was a completely new experience for me—I'd never had a

Prayer is what makes a message powerful and life changing.

new home before, certainly not one of my own. Also, we were starting our family, and Fruitland was an excellent place to raise Andy. But somewhere in my heart I had this understanding that as a servant of God, I had to be ready to go whenever and wherever He called. We could not get so attached to the community or congregation that we would disobey Him.

Sure enough, one day while driving back from Hendersonville's city center, about a hundred yards before I got to the bridge on the Fruitland Road, all of my love for the ministry there completely vanished. I thought, *God, what in the world is going on?* It was such a shock to me—the impression was so strong and overwhelming that I have never forgotten it. My conviction that this was where

God wanted us disappeared—it was totally gone. I didn't really understand what that meant, but I trusted that the Father would show me.

The very next Sunday morning, a pulpit committee from First Baptist Church, Fairborn, Ohio, visited Fruitland Baptist. They stayed after the service to talk to me. They told me that they needed a pastor, and that Ray Roberts, the executive director of the Ohio Baptist Convention, had told them about me. He had been at that Bible Conference at Fruitland that had turned into the powerful and unforgettable prayer meeting, and he was convinced that I was the man for them. Apparently, they were so impressed by Ray's recommendation that they had written to my favorite preaching professor from seminary, Dr. H. C. Brown, and had asked him about me as well. His message back to them was: "If you're talking about the Charles Stanley from Southwestern, get him if you can!" So here they were at Fruitland, to see if I was the man for them.

We spoke, but I made it clear that I was not interested. All they asked was that I pray about it. Naturally, I agreed.

A few days later, I received a formal invitation to be their pastor. But to be frank, their offer couldn't have been less appealing to me. Fairborn was approximately sixty miles between Cincinnati and Columbus. It was too cold in the winter, too hot in the summer, flat, and treeless. No, thank you.

But because I had promised Fairborn's pulpit committee that I would pray about it, I felt compelled to do so. And the more I sought God about it, the more convinced I was that my time in Fruitland was over. The Father was leading Annie and me to serve the church in Fairborn.

At the time, Ohio was a pioneer area for Southern Baptists—there simply wasn't much of a presence there. This fascinated me because it was a wide-open mission field. I thought about what the apostle Paul said: "I aspired to preach the gospel, not where Christ was already named, so that I would not build on another man's foundation; but as it is written, 'They who had no news of Him shall see, and they who have not heard shall understand'" (Rom. 15:20–21). I imagined the excitement and anticipation Paul must have felt when traveling into brand-new areas, proclaiming the Good News that the Messiah had come and that He had provided salvation to all who would believe. Of course, Ohio was far from unreached, but I certainly loved the idea of blazing new trails there.

Likewise, the church was located near Wright-Patterson Air Force Base, so the congregation was primarily military families. Again, this was very attractive to me given my profound appreciation and respect for the men and women in our armed services.

Ultimately, I couldn't deny it. I felt God leading me to accept Fairborn's offer. I knew I had to be open to His plans even if I did not understand them. So on November 8, 1959, I began my tenure as their pastor.

The time at First Baptist Fairborn ended up being a quite challenging. The church was in debt, so we worked hard to pay the bills and build a reservoir of funds. But the spiritual state of some in the congregation was a great deal like its finances. Sadly, some members were trying to achieve God-sized results on their meager human budget of abilities and appeared not to know how to tap in to His treasure of power and wisdom.

As I got to know the church members, I saw that a couple of the deacons seemed desperate to be in control—as many people are. It seemed that the only place they could exert their influence was at church. You can imagine the power struggles that ensued. They often caused trouble in the business meetings and in whatever committees they were on. But the worst part was that they seemed to have trouble relinquishing control to the Lord. They appeared to have no intention of giving their lives to Him or obeying Him.

I prayed diligently for the Father to move there in an extraordinary way and preached my heart out. But nothing moved, which left me incredibly frustrated.

OUT OF THE WILDERNESS, UNTO THE VINE

Thankfully, four good things resulted from our time in Fairborn. First, on June 9, 1961, our daughter Rebecca Louise "Becky" Stanley was born, and of course, that brought us great joy.

Second, I met a lot of young pastors close to my age in Ohio, who struggled with many of the same issues in their churches as I was seeing in mine. Many of them became lifelong friends.

Third, in January 1962, I was asked to travel with a group of seventeen pastors to Haiti on a two-week mission trip. That was an unforgettable experience. I carried Annie's Kodak Retina IIa camera with me and took photos wherever we went. I was absolutely astounded at what I found when we got home and developed those slides—how they captured the experience and the glory of God's creation. I felt as if I'd found a new way to serve and praise the Father. Photography instantly became my favorite hobby. I was fascinated by how everything worked together—light, dark, shutter speed, aperture, focus—like an intricate mathematical equation. And I loved to spend time outdoors, seeing what the Lord was communicating to me through His handiwork.

Fourth, on our way to Haiti, I stopped in Miami to preach at the

First Baptist Church at the invitation of my friend George Folsom, who had some cottages near Fruitland and who occasionally attended services at the church there during the summer. In fact, George had been saved under the ministry in Fruitland and had gotten his life straightened out there. He encouraged the people at First Baptist Miami to invite me, so they did. I agreed to it because my uncle Jack was living in Miami at the time, and he wasn't saved. I wanted more than anything for Jack to know Jesus as his Savior and saw this as an opportunity to reach him.

What an incredibly important morning that turned out to be! Uncle Jack came to services that morning to hear me preach. I could see where he was sitting in the congregation, so I preached my heart out to him for forty-five minutes and looked at him often to see if anything I said was hitting home. Jack did not respond that day, but the church sure did. After that they called me to be their pastor.

I told them I would pray about it, and I did. The problem was that they adored the pastor they'd had before, but he had passed away. They had draped his chair on the platform in black as a memorial to him. That instantly threw up red flags. Would they compare me to him? Would they accept how God would lead me to conduct the business of the church if it was different from how he had handled everything? I prayed throughout the two-week mission trip to Haiti and continued to seek the Lord about it after I got home. The more I prayed, the more I felt that moving to Miami was His will. So I became the pastor of First Baptist Church of Miami on March 18, 1962.

Thankfully, all of my fears were unfounded, and Annie and I absolutely loved every minute of our years in Miami. In fact, in many ways, this new assignment felt like a slice of heaven on earth. The church was growing and Miami was a fantastic place to raise a family. We enjoyed the beach together, rode our bicycles, went to the Orange

Bowl parades and games, and even bought an eighteen-foot Franklin travel trailer. We were all very happy there.

But as time went on, I grew to understand that there was something important missing from my life, but I couldn't identify what it was. I simply felt an underlying restlessness in my spirit.

My uncle Jack did not respond that day, but the church sure did. After that they called me to be their pastor.

We lived just half a block from Biscayne Boulevard, and the church had not only given us a house but also had built me a small concrete-block building with a flat tin roof in the backyard, which became my prayer room and shed. There was a wall down the middle, and on the right side were the lawn mower and tools, and on the left side was my study. I had a door for a desk, some books, and just enough room on the floor so I could pray—stretched out on an afghan my mother had knitted for me. I went out there often. I fasted and sought God as I normally would, trying to understand what He was teaching me and seeking answers wherever I could.

Eventually, it occurred to me that most people go through a crisis of identity in their late twenties and early thirties. It is often during this time that they begin to make the major decisions about who they are going to be and what they will do with their lives. I was thirty-one years old at the time, but I'd never been through such a crisis because my identity had been firmly rooted in Christ from an early age. But as I studied and searched, one thing became increasingly clear to me from reading Scripture: There was much more to this Christian life than I had experienced so far, and I wanted it. Paul's words in Philippians 3:10–11 struck a chord deep within me: The apostle wanted to know Christ, "and the power of His resurrection and the fellowship of His sufferings, being conformed to His death; in order that I may attain to the resurrection from the dead." I yearned for that as well.

I had read about this overflowing resurrection life—the life imbued with the supernatural power of the risen Christ—in a powerful book by Edward McKendree Bounds called *Preacher and Prayer*:

> *The Spirit of God is on the preacher in anointing power, the fruit of the Spirit is in his heart, the Spirit of God has vitalized the man and the word; his preaching gives life, gives life as the spring gives life; gives life as the resurrection gives life; gives ardent life as the summer gives ardent life; gives fruitful life as the autumn gives fruitful life. The life-giving preacher is a man of God, whose heart is ever a thirst for God, whose soul is ever following hard after God, whose eye is single to God, and in whom by the power of God's Spirit the flesh and the world have been crucified and his ministry is like the generous flood of a life-giving river.[9]*

I longed for that kind of deeper walk with the Father characterized by abundant, continuous, and intimate knowledge of His presence and power. I knew what it meant to be filled with the Spirit. I understood what it was to work hard, serve God with all of my heart, and be faithful. But I had never experienced the generous river of the resurrection life that Bounds and Paul spoke of—the kind that could inspire life in others. I knew it was available to me, but I had no idea how to take hold of it in the manner they described (Eph. 1:18–20).

At around that same time, I was preaching through the Book of Galatians, and I'd almost reached the fifth chapter, which is about the fruit of the Holy Spirit. As I studied the passage, I struggled with the fact that my life did not always show the outgrowth that a relationship with Christ should be producing: "love, joy, peace, patience, kindness, goodness, faithfulness, gentleness, self-control" (Gal. 5:22–23). Inherently, I understood that the resurrection life and the fruit of the Spirit were related somehow, but both seemed unattainable for me.

Then came the day I received one of the greatest breakthroughs in my spiritual walk. I remember it as if it were yesterday. It was June 6, 1964, and I was struggling terribly. My heart felt as if it were aching to the point of breaking in two because I felt so defeated. As I went out to pray in my study, I saw a book on the table by the back door. It was titled *They Found the Secret* by V. Raymond Edman. Annie had been to visit her mother, Ethel, in Smithfield, North Carolina, and she'd picked up the book to read on the train home. Somehow, the small volume caught my attention, so I took it with me out to my prayer room.

I stretched out on the floor in that concrete-block shed, and I cried out to the Lord, "Oh God, please, I beg You, give me victory tonight. You've said in Your Word, 'How much more shall the Heavenly Father give the Holy Spirit to them that ask Him' (Luke 11:13). I don't think I can preach publicly again until I get victory. I need continuous, consistent victory, Father. I beg You to search my heart, lay it bare, reveal to me my every sin. Reveal Yourself to me tonight, Lord God. I believe the human heart has no desire that You cannot satisfy. Oh God, out of my heart let the rivers of living water flow."

As I prayed, the Father reminded me of Annie's book. I sat up, opened it to the first chapter, about Hudson Taylor, missionary to China and founder of the China Inland Mission, and began to read.

From the first paragraph, I was hooked: " 'He was a joyous man now, a bright, happy Christian. He had been a toiling, burdened one before, with latterly not much rest of soul. It was resting in Jesus now, and letting Him do the work—which makes all the difference!' Thus spoke a fellow missionary of Hudson Taylor." [10]

"I believe the human heart has no desire that You cannot satisfy. Oh God, out of my heart let the rivers of living water flow."

Toiling, burdened, and without rest of soul—how closely this resembled my own struggle. Yet Taylor had found freedom from that terrible existence. Even from those few first sentences, I knew God had led me to the right place.

Edman went on to say, "Into each life there arises an awareness of failure, a falling short of all that one should be in the Lord." [11] Apparently, what I was experiencing was not as unusual an occurrence in the Christian life as I thought it was. Certainly, Hudson Taylor faced it, too. In a letter to his mother, Taylor echoed my situation in a manner that absolutely astounded me: "I have continually to mourn that I follow at such a distance and learn so slowly to imitate my precious Master. I cannot tell you how I am buffeted sometimes by temptation. I never knew how bad a heart I had. Yet I do know that I love God and love His work, and desire to serve Him only in all things. And I value above all things that precious Savior in Whom alone I can be accepted." [12]

This was exactly what I was going through—I felt completely helpless to change my own heart, even though I wanted to serve God so badly. Perhaps you've felt that way, too. No matter how diligently you try, you keep slipping back into the same bad habits and feel like you're falling short of all God has for you. As the apostle Paul said,

"I am of flesh, sold into bondage to sin. For what I am doing, I do not understand; for I am not practicing what I would like to do, but I am doing the very thing I hate" (Rom. 7:14–15).

Thankfully, God worked through a missionary named John McCarthy to help Taylor through his struggles, which in turn aided me through mine and I pray will assist you through yours.

McCarthy explained that it was not Taylor's duty to sanctify himself—no, it was Christ's work in him that would accomplish what he so deeply desired, which was to be more like Jesus. Taylor's responsibility was simply to abide in Christ and allow the Holy Spirit to do as He so desired. McCarthy wrote,

> *Abiding, not striving nor struggling; looking off unto Him; trusting Him for present power; trusting Him to subdue all inward corruption; resting in the love of an almighty Savior, in the conscious joy of a complete salvation, a salvation "from all sin" (this is His Word); willing that His will should truly be supreme . . . Christ literally all seems to me now the power, the only power for service; the only ground for unchanging joy. May He lead us into the realization of His un-fathomable fullness.*[13]

As I read the excerpt from McCarthy's letter, it was as if a light came on. I had never heard about the abiding life of Christ before this, but it was so clear, so simple. For the first time in my life I began to see the truth that it is not by my effort but by the life of Jesus in me—His life flowing through me by faith—that His kingdom work is accomplished. The concept comes, of course, from John 15:5, where Jesus reveals, "I am the vine, you are the branches; he who abides in Me and I in him, he bears much fruit, for apart from Me you can do nothing." How does a natural branch attached to a vine bear fruit? There is no need for it to do anything, of course; it simply grows. As long as that branch is attached to the vine, it is fed, nourished, and given everything needed for life.

In that instant, I realized that I had been like a branch straining to produce fruit by its own virtue and strength. No wonder I'd been so frustrated. The Holy Spirit didn't just give me power and wisdom for the tasks He wanted me to accomplish case by case. He was actually residing in me and living through me—in every cell, at every moment, actively generating the results He Himself wanted. That truth changed my whole perspective on life and my entire relationship with God.

McCarthy explained that it was Christ's work in him that would accomplish what he so deeply desired.

I wept, overwhelmed with joy that I no longer had to live the Christian life or do ministry in my own strength. All I had to do was simply rest in Jesus and allow Him to do all the work through me.

It was a life-changing moment, which I have never forgotten. I finally understood what Paul meant in Galatians 2:20: "I have been crucified with Christ; and it is no longer I who live, but Christ lives in me; and the life which I now live in the flesh I live by faith in the Son of God, who loved me and gave Himself up for me." I repeated that truth to myself during the next several weeks, etching it into my soul: "It is no longer I who live, but Christ lives in me." His life. His ministry.

The Holy Spirit was residing in me and living through me—in every cell, at every moment, actively generating the results He wanted.

His fruit. From that moment forward, everything in my life was transformed—my preaching, service, leadership, problem solving, relationships—everything. Certainly, Annie noticed the change. I overheard her saying to a friend on the phone, "Something wonderful has happened to Charles. It's like my husband is a different man."

PUTTING IT INTO PRACTICE

Of course, whenever you learn anything new about Christ, God doesn't waste a moment. He immediately sends an opportunity for you to put it into practice.

At the time, I had been reading about George Müller, a godly Christian pastor who founded several New Orphan Houses in Ashley Down, Bristol, and established 117 Christian schools in England. Müller had incredible faith. He knew that because the Lord had called him to serve the orphan community, He would provide everything he needed to operate. So Müller never asked anyone for money—not even a dime. Whenever he was faced with financial needs—and those times were frequent—he went to his knees in prayer, knowing it was an opportunity for his faith to be established. In other words, if the Vine wanted to produce some fruit through the branch, He would provide everything necessary for the branch to do so.

In fact, in his book *A Narrative of Some of the Lord's Dealings with George Müller*, he wrote, "Would the believer, therefore, have his faith strengthened, he must especially give time to God, who tries his faith in order to prove to His child, in the end, how willing He is to help and deliver him, the moment it is good for him." [14]

And the ways God provided for Müller are absolutely beyond imagination. Time and again the Father proved Himself faithful—nothing that the Lord called Müller to do went unfunded. So Müller expressed his unwavering trust in God's provision like this:

Were we to lean upon man, we should surely be confounded; but, in leaning upon the living God alone, we are BEYOND *disappointment, and* BEYOND *being forsaken because of death, or want of means, or want of love, or because of the claims of other work. How precious to have learned in any measure to stand with God alone in the world and yet to be happy, and to know that surely no good thing shall be withheld from us whilst we walk uprightly!* [15]

What a testimony! George Müller's example had an incredible impact on my life. And as I read his amazing story, I felt that God was moving me to open a school there at First Baptist Miami, especially as I read about the influence the schools he established were having reaching children for Christ.

Of course, the very idea of doing so caused me a great deal of trepidation. I didn't know the first thing about how to start a school, organize it, secure funding, hire teachers, choose curriculum, establish guidelines, acquire permits from the local government, recruit students, or anything else that might be required. Likewise, I wasn't sure I could convince the congregation we even needed a school. I felt as if I was not a strong enough branch for the Vine to produce such fruit in me. I was certain I would fail.

But I prayed about it for the next six months, including taking a trip up to George Folsom's cottages in Fruitland with Annie and the children. Annie and I prayed and fasted together during our weeks there. We told Andy and Becky that we were asking God to show us if He wanted our church to have a school by providing the money to pay for it. Then we sought Him together as a family. When we were finished praying, Becky—who was four at the time—went to her room, emptied her piggy bank, put a few pennies, a nickel, and a dime in my hand, and declared that God was already answering our prayers. I was so proud of my little girl!

But the truth of the matter was that when the four of us returned to Miami, I still didn't know how to proceed. A few days later, I was lying on the floor in the sunroom, again praying about the matter. Actually, I was telling the Father how inadequate I felt and all the reasons I was the wrong man to build the school. But God spoke to me very clearly in a manner that showed this was a crucial, defining moment in my life. He said, "Here's your choice. You can do what I tell you and find out what I'll do with you, or you can spend the rest of your life wondering what I would have done if you had obeyed Me." That was all I needed.

So in August 1966, we began classes. And in honor of the great man of faith who had inspired its founding, we called it the George Müeller Christian School. I chose to obey and trust that not only would the Holy Spirit empower us to do all we needed, but that by abiding in Christ, we would see the school flourish. And it certainly did.

Ultimately, my weaknesses and lack of experience weren't important—all that truly mattered was the strength and wisdom of the Vine, the Lord Jesus. The same is true for you. The Savior will always supply and support everything He calls you, the branch, to do. In other words, God will take full responsibility to meet your needs when you obey Him. And He will indeed call

God said, "You can do what I tell you and find out what I'll do with you, or you can spend the rest of your life wondering what I would have done if you had obeyed Me."

you to do things far beyond your abilities and talents so He can make His grace abound in you and show you "that always having all sufficiency in everything, you may have an abundance for every good deed" (2 Cor. 9:8).

COMINGS AND GOINGS

As I said, we loved our years at First Baptist Miami, and I never gave a thought to leaving. I even began my graduate education there—seeking my Th.M. and Th.D. degrees from Luther Rice Seminary.

But one day as I was praying and seeking God, He gave me the strangest verse: "I removed his shoulder from the burden: his hands were delivered from the pots" (Ps. 81:6, KJV). I couldn't stop thinking about it, and I wondered if the Lord was getting me ready to move.

Then one Sunday about three months later, church services were long over, and as I walked out of the church, I found eight people waiting for me. They introduced themselves as a pulpit committee from Bartow, Florida, and they asked if I would mind going to lunch and speaking with them. Annie and I usually had plans after church, but oddly enough, this particular Sunday we didn't have plans to eat with anyone. So I agreed to join them.

During the meal, I assured them that I was happy as a lark in Miami and not interested in leaving. So they began asking what they should be looking for in a pastor. I spent the next three hours describing the kind of man God works through and giving them a list of the questions to ask their candidates.

They listened politely for a long time. Finally, they confessed that they really didn't want anyone else—I was the man for them. Then they told me the story. They'd first visited my church a year before. One of the men explained, "We really liked how you preach. But when you gave the invitation, there was a young fellow who came forward. You got down on your knees beside him and led him to Christ. Well, when we saw that, we knew our church wouldn't be able to handle it. But we've been to fifty-one Southern Baptist churches since then, and no one has been right. God hasn't let us call any of those other preachers we've heard. We know you're what we need."

I really didn't want to leave Miami. But after a visit to Bartow and a couple of months of prayer, it was clear to me that God was once again guiding my steps to serve in a new place.

I began to serve in Bartow in May 1968. Bartow was a typical small county-seat town—full of its own importance and set in its ways. The terrain was hot, flat, and very dull compared to the beauty and atmosphere of Miami. The main attractions there were huge pits where companies had mined for phosphate. When the crews were done mining, they would fill the pits with water; stock them with bluegill, catfish, bass, bream, and carp; and make them into fishing holes. Andy and I could walk from our house to several of these little man-made lakes and spend the day fishing. We enjoyed many a day there together fishing, throwing baseballs, practicing for his Little League games, and teaching him to hunt.

Sadly, the worst part of Bartow was that many of the church members were dry spiritually. They seemed to have little interest in winning anyone to Jesus. As you can imagine, this was incredibly frustrating. I would get ideas for a sermon series and think, *They're not ready for that yet. I'll put that off for a few months.*

But invariably, the Lord would speak directly to my spirit in a manner I wouldn't dare disobey: "No, Charles, preach it *now*." His promptings were insistent and urgent, as if my time there was short.

Turns out, it was. In April 1969, after I had been in Bartow for only eleven months, I went to preach a weeklong revival for a friend in Alexandria, Virginia. Those were some great services—so many people were saved and rededicated their lives to Christ. We were overjoyed with all God was doing.

Oddly, however, every evening I returned to my hotel room feeling very troubled. I was incredibly unsettled, and I didn't know why. So each night I got on my knees and prayed, "God, everything seems to be going well, but something inside of me isn't right. What's going on? Please show me, Father. I've got to find out what's going on."

By Wednesday night, the Lord had given me an idea. I pulled out a yellow legal pad and drew a circle with five lines coming out of it. At the top of each line, I wrote a possibility for the churning I felt within me—trying to get a grasp on what God was getting ready to do. I realized there might be an option that I couldn't imagine, so the last line was simply labeled with a question mark.

- Do something in my life.
- Change me.
- Move me.
- Do something new in my ministry.
- ?

I prayed over each possibility and did the same on Thursday evening as well. Eventually, the Lord's still, small voice answered: "I'm going to move you."

For some reason, I didn't inquire where, I simply asked, "When, Father?" Before my eyes, it was as if a screen appeared—like one you would show a home movie on—and filling it were big, bold, black capital letters: **SEPTEMBER**.

It was such a striking experience that I felt as if I were the prophet Daniel watching the handwriting on the wall.

The vision was burned into my mind, but to be quite frank, it made no sense to me. Leaving Bartow in September meant I would serve the church there for only fifteen months. Surely, God wouldn't move me out of there that quickly, would He? Perhaps the Lord meant September of the

Eventually, the Lord's still, small voice answered: "I'm going to move you."

following year? Was He telling me this almost a year and a half in advance? That didn't sit right either.

But after that, there was no word from God—absolutely nothing. The next night I got on my knees again, but I just couldn't pray. I had no words, and the Father seemed gone, as if He had disappeared.

INTO THE STORM

At home in my study in Bartow at nine that next Monday morning, I received a phone call from my friend Felix Snipes, a music evangelist who'd led worship during revivals at my churches on several occasions. I hadn't heard from him in a couple of years, so we chatted for a while.

Then Felix said something surprising. He said, "Charles, I want to talk to you about something you've never thought about." Of course, I immediately thought about the big question mark I had written on that yellow pad.

He continued, "People here at First Baptist Atlanta have been asking me who I would recommend as an associate pastor for our church, and you're the only person I can think of."

I chuckled. "Now, Felix, I'm certain you could come up with lots of preachers who could fill that position."

He replied, "But you're the only one God keeps bringing to my mind."

I sighed. I knew enough about the pastor of First Baptist Atlanta, Dr. Roy McClain, to know that there was a 180-degree difference in our theological views. In my opinion, he was too liberal in his preaching and in his practices—I would never be comfortable serving with him. I couldn't think of a reason why I should even consider such a demotion.

In fact, I had never even been to Atlanta at that point, so even the city itself had nothing to recommend it. I had only driven through it at various times on my way to North Carolina and Virginia, but I never found a reason to stop.

Naturally, Felix tried to persuade me, but there was no way I would accept. I simply responded, "I just wouldn't be interested in that at all. And besides, I love it here in Bartow. I don't want to leave Florida. We have lots of friends here, and there's a great deal of work to do."

He said, "Well, would you at least pray about it?"

I agreed to pray, but when I hung up the phone, I burst into tears. I could see the pattern the Lord had consistently used throughout my life starting to ramp up again. I thought, *Father, what in the world are You doing? Please don't make me go to Atlanta.*

A couple of weeks later, a pulpit committee showed up in Bartow to speak with me. I told them firmly, "Thank you, but I'm not interested."

They didn't listen. Like an army sent to wear me down, one person after another from First Baptist Atlanta called or showed up in Bartow to try to convince me to change my mind. Each time, I politely but resolutely responded, "No thank you. I have no intention of moving to Atlanta. I'm not interested."

Unfortunately, no matter how hard I tried to close that door, it stayed open. And all the while, I wrestled with what God had said about moving me in September. It occurred to me that September was only a few weeks away, and I hadn't heard from any other churches. First Baptist Atlanta was it—and nothing I seemed to do could drive the opportunity away.

Finally, one of the members of the pulpit committee called and asked, "Can we come down there and take you to lunch?"

I replied, "Well, I hate to see you waste your time or your money. But if you're set on coming, that's fine with me."

On that occasion, eleven people came down to Bartow, including the senior pastor, Dr. Roy McClain. The group made a detailed presentation to me, pulling out all the stops. Still, I didn't find what they had to say very compelling.

When they were done, Dr. McClain asked, "What's your answer?" I could tell by his tone that he was getting impatient.

I replied, "I can't give you an answer."

He was visibly perturbed. "Well, why not?"

I responded, "Because God is going to have to tell me what to do."

"Tell you what to do? What do you think God is going to say to you?" he asked, as if it were a ridiculous notion. I thought to myself, *Lord, do You really want me to go and work under that kind of attitude?*

I answered, "God's going to have to make it absolutely crystal clear that First Baptist Atlanta is His will for me." McClain didn't seem to like that, but he extended an invitation for me to visit Atlanta and see the church campus.

I agreed, but I was very conflicted. As much as I didn't want to go to Atlanta, I couldn't stop praying about it. And one day in prayer, I saw a vision of the skyline of Atlanta with dark, ominous storm clouds hovering over it. I told Annie about it and explained, "I believe that if we go there, it's going to be a rough time." She concurred that a very difficult season appeared to be on the horizon.

As if to confirm my vision, when I visited Dr. McClain in Atlanta, he never looked me in the eye, which sent up red flags. One of my responsibilities would be to preach on Sunday nights, so it was obvious to me that theological and doctrinal clashes were ahead for us. I asked him flat out, "Suppose you preach one thing on Sunday morning and I preach something else on Sunday night. What would happen then?"

He replied, "Well, I won't pour you into my mold; just don't expect to pour me into yours." I was speechless. I couldn't understand such a seeming lack of conviction. We were wholly incompatible, and I wondered how a church could survive being divided in such a manner.

To make matters worse, about a week later, one of my good friends—who was a pastor in Miami at the time—came to see me in Bartow. He said, "Charles, I've come here to tell you why you shouldn't go to First Baptist Atlanta. I want to protect you from going there because no good can come of it." He then proceeded to disclose details about the church that were very unsettling.

"I believe that if we go to Atlanta, it's going to be a rough time."

When he left, I fell to my knees in prayer. I could not believe the Father would send me into such a mess. But the Lord said to me, "Are you going to listen to him or are you going to trust Me?"

What was I supposed to say? Of course I would listen to God. But why would He lead me into such a difficult situation?

These are the moments that define what a person really believes. The warning signs are crystal clear, and we can see that only adversity lies ahead. And yet we know that God is directing us to turn into the storm. What we decide at these times ultimately shapes our futures in ways we can never imagine.

Personally, I felt as if the Lord had been preparing me for this all my life. Through each move He'd called me to, the Lord had matured, shaped, and taught me for this moment. I had already decided that I wanted to be the type of person who would fly into the tempest, the kind of believer who would trust the Lord regardless of the challenges. And, naturally, I recalled my grandfather's advice about brick walls.

Undoubtedly, that's what the apostle Paul did. As he made his way to Jerusalem on his final missionary journey, he was warned repeatedly about the persecution ahead. He knew that only hardship and death awaited him. Yet Paul courageously declared, "Behold, bound by the Spirit, I am on my way to Jerusalem, not knowing what will happen to me there, except that the Holy Spirit solemnly testifies to me in every city, saying that bonds and afflictions await me. But I do not consider my life of any account as dear to myself, so that I may finish my course and the ministry which I received from the Lord Jesus, to testify solemnly of the gospel of the grace of God" (Acts 20:22–24).

And when Paul's friends begged him not to go, as my friend had pleaded with me, he replied, "I am ready not only to be bound, but even to die at Jerusalem for the name of the Lord Jesus" (Acts 21:13). Certainly, that was the kind of courage I wanted to characterize my life as well. If Paul had been prepared to die for Jesus—who gave His life for all of us—I should at the very least be willing to suffer for Him.

So, finally, I prayed, "Father, if You really want me to go to Atlanta, I'll go. I will do whatever You ask of me." And by September 30, 1969, we were moving to Georgia.

I hope that if you ever come to such a crossroad in your life, you will do the same. Because immediately after I submitted to the Father, the inner churning I'd felt for months ceased, and the peace of God, which transcends all understanding, washed over me. And I knew that regardless of the battles I faced, He would be with me—just as He will be with you.

RIGHT AT HOME

Of course, the first hurdle I would have to overcome in going to First Baptist Atlanta was how it would affect my family. Annie already supported the decision; she had been praying about it right along with me.

I wanted to find out how Andy and Becky felt about it, because they loved Bartow and had lots of friends there. Likewise, it meant uprooting them from schools they'd only recently started attending. I didn't want them to feel as if they had no part in the direction the family was taking—because ultimately, I knew that would shape how they saw God. Rather, I wanted them to be part of any decisions we made as a family. There was safety and security in that. Even if they didn't get their way, they'd know they'd been heard, just as the Father always listens to us when we seek Him. So whenever any big moves, changes, or choices arose, I would explain all of the circumstances to the degree they could understand them, and we would pray about the decision together.

One night, as we often did, the four of us went on a bicycle ride— Andy and I were riding up front and Annie and Becky were following along behind us.

Andy was eleven at the time, and I asked him, "Andy, what would you say if I told you God was calling us to a big city to serve at another church? If we moved, you would have to change schools and we might not be able to live in as nice a house as we have now because I would be the associate pastor—so it would be a sacrifice. How would you feel about that?"

Andy thought for a moment and then said, "Well, Dad, every time God has told us to do something and we've done it, He's blessed us more than we expected. So if God has called us to go, He'll take care of us."

I nearly fell off my bicycle. I thought to myself, *Hallelujah! I must be doing something right!* As parents, we're always teaching our children something by how we live and respond to situations. They either believe our lifestyle is worthy of imitation, or they don't. I was thrilled that Andy was committed enough to Christ at such a young age, that he was willing to obey, even if that meant giving up things that were important to him. That delighted me more than I can express. He understood that if we obeyed God, we could leave all the consequences to Him. Somehow he had seen it in our lives and found it worth emulating.

Naturally, in all the fields of service the Lord has led me to throughout the years, my very favorite and the most important to me has been my family. It's moments like those with Andy and Becky that have filled me with the greatest joy and sense of fulfillment.

As you can imagine, Annie and I were thrilled beyond measure when they were born. From the moment I saw them, I fell completely in love with them. I had never seen anything so beautiful as those little faces. They awakened emotions in me that I had never experienced before. I sensed a deep awareness of the responsibility I bore toward them as their teacher, protector, and provider, and I also felt a new appreciation for the love our heavenly Father has toward us as His children.

This was surprising to me.

"Dad, every time God has told us to do something and we've done it, He's blessed us more than we expected. So if God has called us to go, He'll take care of us."

Holding them in my arms for the first time, the weight of my role in their lives overwhelmed me, as did the love I felt for them. I had a profound desire to instruct and safeguard them in the very best way possible. And I wanted to make sure every decision I made on their behalf was absolutely right.

In fact, Andy was three days old before I gave him a name. Annie and I already had a girl's name picked out—if we had a daughter, we were naming her after my mother, Rebecca. But I had no idea about what to call our son. When time drew near to bring him home from the hospital, Annie looked at me and said, "Honey, we've got to put a name on this boy."

It seemed like such a tremendous decision—choosing what he would be called for the rest of his life. In Hebrew culture, a name is very important because it says a great deal about the character of the person who bears it. I felt that even in this first decision on my son's behalf, I had an opportunity to shape his future in a positive way. So that night I got the Bible out. I prayed, "Okay, Lord, show me what to call him."

I started reading in the Gospel of John and I came across the name Andrew. It was a name I liked, so I opened the concordance and began to track the apostle Andrew's life. What I found was that every time Andrew is mentioned in the Bible, He is serving the Lord Jesus and bringing people to Him. Interestingly, the name Andrew means "manly" in Greek. What an excellent object lesson from this apostle's life: What characterized a true man was his service and commitment to the Savior. I knew right there and then, that was our son's name.

That profound love and sense of responsibility carried over to every decision we made in regard to Andy and Becky's upbringing. Annie and I prayed over them constantly, thanking the Lord for the privilege of being entrusted with them and acknowledging that they belonged to Him first and foremost. I praise God that both of them trusted in Jesus as their Savior when they were five years old.

After all, if there's something you'd want to leave someone you love, it's the one thing they cannot lose. Thankfully, as my mother had done for me, I knew that I could turn to Scripture for wisdom about positively influencing my children to love the Lord and serve others. In fact, for me, fatherhood was the prime opportunity to put God's Word into action.

Apparently, my practice of putting God first affected their lives powerfully. Years ago, as I was preparing to teach a parenting series,

For me, fatherhood was the prime opportunity to put God's Word into action.

I asked Andy and Becky to tell me what stuck with them as they were growing up. To my amazement, they both mentioned prayer and how from early on they'd learned that they are ultimately responsible to God for the choices they make. You can imagine the joy it gave me to hear my children say this.

Of course, from the time they were teenagers, whenever they came to me for advice about anything, instead of telling them what I thought, I would say: "Have you asked God about that? What has He told you to do?" And I would remind them that in Psalm 32:8 He promises, "I will instruct you and teach you in the way which you should go; I will counsel you with My eye upon you."

I knew that sometimes frustrated them. It took a lot more work to seek the Lord than to have me direct them in what choices to make. They would say, "Oh, Dad! We want to know what you think! Can't you just tell us?" But I wouldn't budge. As tempting as it was to take the lead, it was important for them to learn to listen to God for themselves and make their own mistakes.

I will admit that wasn't always easy. At times, they'd head down the wrong path and would ask my opinion about their course. I didn't want to impede them from learning valuable lessons, but I also longed to protect them from making mistakes that would impact their futures. So I would say, "Keep praying about it," or I would suggest, "Let's get the Bible and find out what God says." I trusted that the Lord would straighten it out, and He always did. Eventually, Becky and Andy knew how to turn to God and His Word as they sought to make the right decisions.

I didn't want to impede my children from learning valuable lessons, but I also longed to protect them from making mistakes that would impact their futures.

Annie and I made family dinner a priority, and we ate together almost every night. Likewise, as I said previously, we periodically had family meetings in which we talked about big decisions, shared what God was doing in our lives, discussed chores, and made plans for special events and vacations. We spent as much quality time together as we could. I've already mentioned some of the things we did—fishing, hiking, playing board games and cards, hunting, attending sporting events, and what have you. I made a point to engage in as many fun activities with them as our budget would allow.

For example, when we lived in Miami, we toured a World War II submarine and rode the Goodyear Blimp. Likewise, we took an extended trip at least once a year in our eighteen-foot Franklin travel trailer, which we pulled behind the car. We loved to go to Naples, Florida, which was right across the state from the church in Miami. At that time, we could actually pull up on the pristine beach and set up a campsite. We would have a grand time enjoying campfires, collecting seashells, and going snorkeling. On one occasion, we got truly ambitious and pulled that trailer across the country all the way to California. It took five weeks, but we saw the Grand Canyon, Yosemite, and everything the great American West had to offer.

Of course, to this day, Andy and Becky will tell you that five weeks is far too long for any family to spend together in such a confined space. But those were times when we could simply be together and enjoy each other. To me, it didn't actually matter what we were doing as long as the four of us were together. What I loved most about being with them was the conversations we had. I listened with great interest to their thoughts and discoveries, and I was careful to watch for op-portunities to teach them about God and to help them deepen the intimate relationship they had with Him.

When I look at them today, and see the ways they are living for Jesus and parenting their own kids, I feel profound satisfaction. Even as a teenager, Andy would tell me, "When I have a son, I'm going to tell him the same thing you keep telling me because of how much it encouraged me and helped me stay on the right track. For years you've said, 'Andy, God loves you, and I believe He has something special for you. God has a plan for your life, and you don't want to miss it.' "

That's exactly what I had always tried to teach him: "Andy, you are somebody, you are loved, and you have unlimited potential to affect eternity," and it made a difference in his life.

The most wonderful part is that on September 23, 2012, when I turned eighty, Andy again reminded me of the influence of this powerful principle. He had written it down as a commitment in his journal on September 29, 1975: "I need to tell my boy at a young age that God told me He was going to use my son in a great way." And indeed, he and his wife, Sandra, have instilled into their children's lives the truth that the Lord has a wonderful plan for them. The same is true for Becky and her children.

As I think of all the years we've had and all the trials we've been though together, I would say that I couldn't be more proud of Andy, Becky, and my grandchildren, and all the Father has done in and through them. What an extraordinary blessing to see my children obeying God's Word and seeing my grandchildren likewise serving the Savior.

WHEREVER YOU ARE, SERVE GOD

The point is: How the Lord works through you in this world isn't always how you'd expect Him to. Ministry can happen on foreign shores with people who don't even communicate in your language as well as right in your own home with those who share your surname.

Wherever you are is where God wants you to shine the light of the truth.

At times, the Father will call you to places where it's easy to see the fruit of your labor and where you'll receive great fulfillment from

I couldn't be more proud of Andy, Becky, and my grandchildren, and all the Father has done in and through them.

your work. But at other times, you may experience a great deal of adversity and have no idea what God is up to. Regardless of the situation, your responsibility is to keep seeking and serving Him faithfully, trusting that He

has incredible things that He wants to accomplish through you and that He will not fail to bring them about (Ps. 57:2).

The Lord created you with a unique mix of personality, gifts, and talents to represent Him in a very special way. And because you have been bought by the blood of Jesus, empowered by the Holy Spirit, instructed through His Word, and given His resurrection life, you can be confident that you have everything you need to succeed in every good work He commissions you to carry out—even the most challenging ones. This is because He is the Vine and you are the branch. He is the One who produces the fruit; your responsibility is simply to abide in Him (John 15:5).

But it is also immensely important for you to realize that the Father will work through the places where He leads you to serve in order to mature *you* spiritually. In every church God led me to—Fruitland, Fairborn, Miami, Bartow, and Atlanta—He had lessons for me to learn and crucial ways He was preparing me for the next step. He will do the same for you.

In fact, you may benefit as much as—if not more than—those

whom you serve whenever you obey God. Why? Because when you stay in the center of His will, you grow in Christ's likeness and live out the reason for which you were created. Ministering to others in Jesus' name gives you opportunities to exercise your spiritual gifts and demonstrate the principles of Scripture with your life. Yes, at times it will be extremely difficult, there will be spiritual warfare, and you will see no light ahead. It won't feel as if anything good is coming from your suffering. But you can absolutely count on the fact that God will use every bit of the adversity for your good and His glory if you will abide in Him and continue to trust Him (Rom. 8:28).

As I said earlier, ministry is never what you imagine it will be. And even when it is demanding and disheartening, it is still better than any other activity you can engage in because you are serving the eternal God who is producing everlasting fruit through you (Phil. 1:6). You can be certain that no matter how your situation or circumstance appears here on earth, everything you do in obedience to Him is like a treasure you've stored up in heaven (Matt. 6:19–21).

Hebrews 6:10 promises, "God is not unjust so as to forget your work and the love which you have shown toward His name, in having ministered and in still ministering to the saints." Even the most seemingly insignificant tasks you do out of love and submission to Him—such as giving someone a cup of cool water to

> *Everything you do in obedience to Him is like a treasure you've stored up in heaven.*

drink (Matt. 10:42)—are accounted for and blessed beyond measure.

So my challenge to you is to keep all this in mind as you go about your day. You may have many unpleasant responsibilities to take care of, but do them for God—as if He is your boss. The Father has an important plan and purpose for your life, and you have absolutely no idea about all He wants to accomplish in and through you. You have unlimited potential to affect eternity. So serve Him by faithfully carrying out whatever He calls you to do, cling to Him in prayer, seek Him through His Word, turn into the storms, love others in His name, and look for opportunities to teach everyone you meet about an intimate relationship with God. Because there is absolutely no better use of your time here on earth, and, certainly, He is and always will be "a rewarder of those who seek Him" (Heb. 11:6).

MY FATHER, MY FRIEND

by Becky Stanley Brodersen

Fathers and daughters. The trickiest combination in a family. The relationship can be many things—loving, tumultuous, fiercely loyal, exasperating—but it is never neutral. Any father and daughter can survive adolescence and the teenage years as long as unconditional love rules the day. Dad never lost sight of that, and I'm grateful to God he didn't.

From as far back as I can remember, Dad and I had the kind of relationship that describes two people who meet for the first time and feel like they've known each other for years. The same ingredient in him has always been in me, and the only way I know to describe it is Becca, his mom, my grandmother. I was named after Becca, and once that was decided, I took on more than just her name, which means "loyal." Like Becca, Dad and I had more in common than getting up early. We liked to talk about many of the same subjects. Neither of us was much good at small talk, and we shared a comfortable familiarity that only increased as the years went by.

When I was five years old, I was faced with an important decision. I had attended two years of kindergarten where the Bible was taught from cover to cover. I had heard dozens of sermons while sitting in the second row on Sunday mornings. And I had been a part of countless family powwows where I had witnessed many answers to prayer. It was time I met God personally. The weight of the decision

rested heavily upon me. I understood how to be saved and
why I needed to be, but I didn't want to "come to Jesus"
alone.

I don't know if it was all those early morning bike rides
on Dad's handlebars or if it was all the games of Rook he and
I won on vacation or if it was his willingness to be my dance
partner when he came home from work, but on the morning
that I decided to ask Jesus into my heart, Dad was the one
I wanted to pray with. After breakfast we knelt by my bed.
Dad began to pray, and I began to weep. When it was my
turn, I could barely speak. I remember Dad being especially
patient while I talked to God about my sin. When it was all
over, I was relieved, but I also felt vulnerable. I had just given
up control of my life to Someone I couldn't see. Dad and I
had discussed my decision beforehand to make sure I understood what I was doing, so afterward, he didn't say much.
He just hugged me with big tears in his eyes. You never forget
who was present when you were saved. For me, there was no
one but Dad.

We did not always see eye to eye on everything, however,
and I was often the first to call it. I am not sure what gave me
the confidence or the foolhardiness to be so frank with Dad.
Maybe it was that shared substance I can't quite name. I just
know that growing up, I prevailed upon his unconditional
love for me more than he deserved and I learned a powerful
lesson about parenting without realizing it. Regardless of
my behavior, he kept his drawbridge down with the letters
G-R-A-C-E written on each plank. Dad never held a grudge,
and he was always quick to forgive.

I credit Dad's steady heart to all those hours on his knees, alone with God, his Bible, and Becca's afghan.

That's the way I will always remember Dad—praying. Dad's model for life was simple: Make prayer your practice, make trust your posture, and make obedience your pattern— and NEVER waver.

Dad's faith in God was so real you could almost touch it. All that time he spent in the Word and on his knees created a calm confidence in him that buffered him for the years ahead. I'm sorry to say that I walked through Dad's dark night of the soul with him from a distance. Marriage, children, and a cross-country move were part of the reason. But there were other forces at work, and the threads of our relationship were tested. I have come to know that when God plans to use a person in someone's life down the road, the enemy often does his best to sabotage the relationship beforehand. I can look back now and see how that was taking place. But God, being God, took Dad's trial and used it for good not only in his life but also in mine. I watched as he accepted what God allowed to occur in his life and the forgiveness he extended toward those involved. As time passed, I saw changes in my dad, *good* changes, and it became true of him like it was for Joseph, "God meant it for good" (Gen. 50:20).

On the day I called Dad with sad news about my own circumstances, his first words were, "Becky, I'm sorry you did not feel free to tell me sooner." That was not his fault, but mine. There was no sermon and no judgment, only love and understanding. It's one thing to walk through adversity with a church member. But it is something completely different

* * *

when it's your own daughter. Dad was nothing but kindness, patience, and gentleness throughout an unusually dark period of my life. He spent countless hours with me on the phone. And we shed many tears together. Time and time again, I saw how God had mercifully prepared Dad to walk through my grief and sorrow with me like no one else could.

My goal for writing was not to tell you all the lessons Dad taught me. What I want you to know is that Dad lived what he taught. There's the rub with dads and daughters. The world may see one side of a person and be fooled. But a daughter is never fooled. A daughter expects nothing less than authenticity. If a dad won't produce the real stuff of life, the daughter suffers and their relationship never flourishes.

It takes courage to become authentic. It also takes humility. Dad learned those traits from Becca. Becca, who had no earthly inheritance to leave Dad, but she left him wealthy nonetheless.

It's funny how that works. I don't know what happened to my first bike or my first stereo, but I still know the Person Dad introduced me to when I was five. And I still read the same Book that stayed open on Becca's old afghan where Dad prayed. And like Dad, I get up early in the morning to start my day with God.

I consider myself fortunate to have had Dad as a father. But what I am especially grateful for is that through everything he has become my dearest friend as well.

6

Battles

Crowns and thrones may perish, kingdoms rise and wane,
But the church of Jesus constant will remain.
Gates of hell can never 'gainst that church prevail;
We have Christ's own promise, and that cannot fail.
Onward, Christian soldiers, marching as to war,
With the cross of Jesus going on before.
—Sabine Baring-Gould, 1865

"The Lord gets His best soldiers
out of the highlands of affliction."
—Charles Spurgeon

If you've been a Christian for any length of time, you've probably noticed that not everybody is going to comprehend your desire to obey God and follow Jesus. In fact, the reality is that very few people will. When you are truly living for the Savior, you are pretty much guaranteed that there will be times you will be misunderstood and mistreated. Others may not appreciate your commitment to the Lord and may even actively oppose you because of it.

Jesus said it Himself: "I have chosen you out of the world. That is why the world hates you. Remember what I told you: 'A servant is not greater than his master.' If they persecuted me, they will persecute you also" (John 15:19–20).

This is because the world and its system rejects Christ as the true and rightful King of all that exists (Phil. 2:9–11; Rev. 19:16). Psalm 2:2–3 tells us, "The rulers take counsel together against the LORD and against His Anointed, saying, 'Let us tear their fetters apart and cast away their cords from us!' " Inherently, the fallen, sinful nature within mankind fights to throw off the rulership of God. So when you commit yourself to Christ, accepting the Lord's rightful authority, you will find yourself in opposition to the world (1 Cor. 2:14). Jesus did well to warn us, "You will be hated by all because of My name" (Luke 21:17).

Of course, this is never easy to swallow. It may be understandable when the antagonism comes from other religions, governments, or secular sources because a natural rivalry exists for people's hearts and minds. But attacks that come from other Christians—who are supposed to be our brothers and sisters in the faith—can be especially difficult to accept. After all, we are supposed to be the *Body* of Christ, unified and working together to make His name known among the nations (John 17:22–23). And we are commanded, "Seek to abound for the edification of the church" (1 Cor. 14:12). Yet the Christian army has become infamous for shooting its own soldiers and for perpetual conflict. Why is this? I think there are several reasons.

FIRST, SOMETIMES PEOPLE SINCERELY BELIEVE SOMETHING DIFFERENT. For example, during the time the Church was being established, some believed that the Gentiles—or non-Jews—who were being saved should live by all the Jewish commandments. But others said Jesus had set them free from the Law and that the Gentiles shouldn't be expected to observe it. In other words, the question they were debating was: Apart from accepting the free gift of salvation, are followers of Christ expected to also follow the Law?

This was a big deal. It not only affected new believers in terms of what was considered acceptable in their dietary and behavioral habits, it also included questions such as whether or not Christian men should be circumcised. So the leaders at the church in Jerusalem held a council to discuss the issue (Acts 15). It turns out that both groups had some valid points (vv. 19–29). These early believers did not set out to hurt one another; rather, they discussed their differences in order to come to a deeper understanding of Christ and for the good of the Church.

Fruitful discussion is possible when both parties base their understanding on the Word of God and submit to the Holy Spirit, who brings unity (Eph. 4:1–6). Unfortunately, many of the conflicts that arise in the Church are based not on Scripture but on people's experiences and preferences—and that is when the real problems begin.

SECOND, CONFLICTS OFTEN OCCUR IN THE CHURCH BECAUSE BE-LIEVERS ARE ENVIOUS OF GOD'S ANOINTING ON A PERSON'S LIFE AND THE AUTHORITY ASSOCIATED WITH IT. This was certainly true in Paul's case. He spoke of those who "proclaim Christ out of selfish ambition rather than from pure motives, thinking to cause me distress in my imprisonment" (Phil. 1:17). Those people wanted Paul's power and influence in the churches but had no understanding of what it cost him to establish them (2 Cor. 11:23–33).

You will see this in every area of life. There are blessings that come with God's call on your life that others will want for themselves. They will believe they can have them by undermining or using you—never realizing that those gifts are not simply for the taking. Rather, they are from the Lord to those who are faithful to Him.

THIRD, SOMETIMES THE ENEMY WORKS THROUGH PEOPLE'S WOUNDEDNESS TO CAUSE DIVISION IN THE CHURCH. There are instances when people are driven not by selfish ambition or vain conceit but by ingrained feelings of inferiority and rejection. The enemy then works through their damaged emotions to create chaos in the Church. It is so important to pray for those who persecute us, no matter their motives (Matt. 5:44). In fact, the Father may put these people in our lives so that we can help them. This is why Paul admonishes, "The LORD's bond-servant must not be quarrelsome, but be kind to all, able to teach, patient when wronged,

When conflicts arise and someone is acting out, get on your knees, pray for that person, and ask God if there is any way He wants you to help him.

with gentleness correcting those who are in opposition, if perhaps God may grant them repentance leading to the knowledge of the truth, and they may come to their senses and escape from the snare of the devil, having been held captive by him to do his will" (2 Timothy 2:24–26).

Our goal should always be to see people freed from their sins, healed from their wounds, and filled with faith in Christ, so that they can escape the strongholds of the enemy, the unity of the church can be maintained, and God can be glorified. So when conflicts arise and someone is acting out, get on your knees, pray for that person, and ask God if there is any way He wants you to help him (Matt. 18:15–17; Luke 6:27–35).

FINALLY, CONFLICTS OCCUR IN THE CHURCH BECAUSE SOME
PEOPLE WHO CLAIM TO BE BELIEVERS IN FACT DO NOT HAVE A
TRUE, ABIDING RELATIONSHIP WITH JESUS. You will find that in
your own congregation there may be people who are Christian by
their culture—saying and doing what *seem* to be the right things—
but they are far from allowing Jesus to be the Lord of their lives.
You can identify them by what is produced in and through them
(Matt. 7:20–21). Instead of being characterized by the honorable and
praiseworthy fruit of the Spirit, their words and actions are selfish,
sinful, and divisive (Gal. 5:19–23).

Jesus talks about this in the Parable of the Wheat and the Tares
(Matt. 13:24–30), where the enemy sows destructive weeds into a
man's fields in order to destroy the harvest. In much the same way,
the enemy plants people in the church who don't really have a relationship with Christ in order to devastate other believers, spread
false doctrine, cause discord, and undermine the work of the gospel
in the world. We must do everything we can to reach these people for
Jesus, but if they will not be moved, we must take the proper steps
to ensure the unity and health of the congregation (Matt. 18:15–17;
2 John 1:7–10).

IS PEACE POSSIBLE?

In light of this, can we still have peace in the midst of all the conflicts?
Absolutely. Philippians 4:6–7 promises, "Be anxious for nothing,
but in everything by prayer and supplication with thanksgiving let
your requests be made known to God. And the peace of God, which
surpasses all comprehension, will guard your hearts and your minds
in Christ Jesus." Here, the Greek word for *guard* means to "garrison

you about, hem you in, and protect by a military sentinel." As you walk in His will, the Lord encompasses you as your Protector and Provider—and no one can break through His defenses. The Father encircles you with His own matchless presence, and the only way anything can get to you is if He Himself opens the door and allows it. That is the greatest security you and I could ever ask for.

Understanding this is the most powerful weapon in your arsenal as a believer and the reason you can remain at peace when conflicts and accusations are flying about. You can know for certain that the Lord your God safeguards you. You are anchored to the Son of God, and He is immovable, steadfast, and strong on your behalf.

The only way anything can get to you is if God Himself opens the door and allows it.

I have traveled to many places on this earth, and nowhere was this truth about God's peace more evident than in the tumultuous land of Israel. I was actually there while the Israelis were in the middle of the 1982 Lebanon War. Many people who had signed up for the tour had canceled, worried about their safety in the midst of such a bitter conflict. Yet I found it to be the most peaceful and remarkable place I have ever been. The Lord's presence there was unmistakable.

Our tour group was told that missiles were being fired into the area around Capernaum on the northern shore of the Sea of Galilee, where Jesus established His headquarters and did a great deal of His ministry. But when we were there, we were confident that our God was greater than anything the enemy could throw at us. In fact, I didn't feel even a twinge of fear. Instead, I looked at the ruins of the synagogue where Jesus had taught and performed miracles and knew that God had called me to be in that sacred place where my Savior had stood. The awe of it encompassed me, and I felt His presence in such a powerful way that nothing could disturb it. But that is what you will always find—the absolute safest place in the world is in the center of God's will, no matter what else is going on around you.

Then I recalled Christ's promise in John 14:27, "Peace I leave with you; My peace I give to you; not as the world gives do I give to you. Do not let your heart be troubled, nor let it be fearful." Jesus doesn't give tranquility as the world does. The world's peace is temporary, and you can experience it only when everything is quiet and going your way. But the peace that Jesus gives is meant to be embraced in the midst of the battles and storms, when everything seems to be going wrong and help seems far away.

How true it was that day in Israel—a war was waging around us and yet in the places where the Savior had performed His ministry, our little group felt such a profound sense of His awesome power and protection. We were confident that

> *The peace that Jesus gives is meant to be embraced in the midst of the battles and storms, when everything seems to be going wrong and help seems far away.*

no matter how real or terrifying the danger, our Almighty God was greater than anything the enemy could throw at us. As Jesus said in John 16:33, "These things I have spoken to you, so that in Me you may have peace. In the world you have tribulation, but take courage; I have overcome the world."

And so this is how we face any conflict or tempest that arises. We stay as close to the Savior as we can, walk in the center of His will, and trust Him to be our Defender—confident that He can overcome anything that assails us.

A BATTLE FOR THE SOUL
OF THE CHURCH

I surely needed the assurance of God's peace in the midst of tribulation when I went to First Baptist Atlanta (FBA). As I said in the previous chapter, I knew dark times were ahead. In fact, I complained every mile of the road from Bartow, Florida, to Atlanta, Georgia, because of how difficult I knew it would be to deal with the liberal senior pastor, rampant church politics, and my demotion to associate pastor. But God had directed me to go, so I reluctantly obeyed.

When I actually started work on October 12, 1969, it wasn't as bad as I'd thought it would be—it was ten times worse. Nobody at the church other than the executive committee and the handful of staff members sent to recruit me knew I was coming. They certainly weren't ready for me. One fellow ushered me into a small office that didn't even have a desk. When I asked about it, the man indicated that I would just have to deal with it—he was unwilling to find a desk or purchase one for me. Finally, one of the deacons volunteered to lend me a desk, but all the drawers were locked and no one knew where the key was.

Talk about feeling unwanted. I would periodically hear the snide remark, "Can anything good come out of Bartow, Florida?" Sadly, most of the church members seemed cold and unwelcoming—even the building's appearance was uninviting. The carpet was ragged and the walls were a depressing dark green color—the whole place seemed old, dark, and decaying.

The way I was introduced to the church didn't help either. On my first Sunday morning, a man stood up and said, "I want you to meet our new associate pastor, Charles Stanley. He's going to preach for us this morning." That was it. No vote of confidence. No support. All the appreciation and respect I'd been shown by the leaders of FBA as they tried to recruit me were gone. What remained was a "You're nobody—do as you're told!" attitude that infected every aspect of the church.

I quickly discovered that this mind-set emanated from seven very powerful men on the executive committee who ran the church. These men were accustomed to calling all the shots. There were sixty deacons as well, but most of them seemed unengaged—merely there for social, political, and business reasons. This small group of power brokers and their allies kept an iron-tight grip on everything that went on in the church. Worst of all, they appeared to have absolutely no interest in what God had to say about it. Deep in my spirit I knew the Lord wanted His church back and that's why He'd brought me there.

I'd been at FBA only three months when this was confirmed in a mighty way. It was January 1970, and my friend Stephen Olford came to preach at the Georgia Baptist Convention Evangelism Conference, which was being hosted at FBA. That morning, Dr. Olford's message was about the Holy Spirit and how He works to redeem humanity. It was powerful. But it also showed me how far FBA was out of God's will. In my mind, there was no way to deny the Father's displeasure with the church's condition—ruled by men rather than the Savior who had redeemed her.

As I listened to the invitation hymn, "Have Thine Own Way, Lord," by Adelaide A. Pollard, God was stirring a conviction in me in such an overwhelming way that all I wanted to do was get out of there so I could pray.

Have Thine own way, Lord! Have Thine own way!
Thou art the Potter, I am the clay.
Mold me and make me, after Thy will,
While I am waiting, yielded and still . . .

Have Thine own way, Lord! Have Thine own way!
Hold o'er my being absolute sway!
Fill with Thy Spirit till all shall see
Christ only, always, living in me.

Each word was a call to arms. I knew God was enlisting me to do spiritual battle for the church. So as soon as the invitation was over, I rushed to my office and told the secretary, "Don't let anyone in here."

For the next two hours, I stayed stretched out before the Father, and He revealed a glimpse of what I was going to face. It was as if He were saying, "I'm getting you ready, Charles. Here's what you can expect." Sadly, it was all bad—the road ahead was marked with terrible conflict and spiritual warfare. When I was done praying, I was physically and emotionally spent.

Yet I knew that the Father was showing me the reality of the situation so I would be prepared for the challenges before me. As Amos 3:7 teaches, "Surely the LORD GOD does nothing unless He reveals His secret counsel to His servants the prophets." No wonder the Lord had been unmistakably clear in the vision He had given me in that hotel room in Alexandria, Virginia. He had revealed that He was moving me in such a powerful way so I wouldn't have any doubts that this was indeed His will for me. And now He was giving me this confirmation so I would be filled with purpose and resolve for the battles ahead and not be discouraged.

And I am glad He did. I was tasked with preaching on Sunday

and Wednesday nights, as well as working with the youth and college students, along with a lady who would become a faithful friend, Mary Gellerstedt. Thankfully, people started attending those Sunday and Wednesday services and accepting Christ as their Savior. The church began to grow. I was humbled to hear people make statements such as, "I've learned more about the Word of God in the last six months than I have in my entire life." I was grateful for God's confirmation that I was on the right track.

But that ruling committee of seven men made it exceedingly clear that they did not approve of my bib-

God made sure I didn't have any doubts that this was indeed His will for me.

lically conservative and evangelistic style of preaching. In fact, they accused me of being unable to preach anything but how to be saved, the Holy Spirit, and the return of Christ. So early on, those men put pressure on me to quit. In time I came to believe they had hired me for the sole purpose of replacing Dr. McClain, but I was proving harder to control than they'd expected.

It was then that I began to understand Dr. McClain a little better. He had been at FBA for sixteen years and had been living under their regime for a very long time—struggling with their attempts to micromanage his every move. I still didn't agree with all of his theology or practices, but it became clear why he didn't oppose their efforts to hire an associate pastor with such different beliefs. Dr. McClain was seldom at the church—I'd seen him there only three times apart from Sunday morning services. I imagine that those seven men were actively pressuring him to resign and that after facing their brutal assaults for so long, he had finally lost the will to fight them.

But the last straw for Dr. McClain came in September 1970, when FBA had an evangelist come in for a weeklong revival at the church and no one was saved or came forward to make a decision. At the end of the week, McClain preached a message, and still no one responded to the invitation. He looked out at the congregation in disgust and shouted, "This is so sickening, I can't stand it! I'm through!" He threw the microphone down on the platform, walked out, and resigned soon thereafter.

GOD'S BATTLEGROUND

With Dr. McClain gone, I was asked to preach on Sunday mornings, which I did. That was when my real troubles at FBA began. As acting pastor, I would sit in on business meetings with the group of seven, where they indicated in no uncertain terms that they had absolutely no interest in my opinion. But I wasn't too concerned with what they thought because I knew I had a biblical responsibility to the congregation—the same responsibility Paul declared to the church at Colossae: "Of this church I was made a minister according to the stewardship from God bestowed on me for your benefit, so that I might fully carry out the preaching of the word of God" (Col. 1:25). As the church's spiritual leader, I was entrusted to set a godly example—and that was what I was resolved to do.

I still remember that first business meeting after Dr. McClain left as if it were this morning. We were discussing some point of contention, and I said, "We need to ask God about this."

One of the men immediately replied, "This is business. Leave God out of it." Those men absolutely refused to pray about it.

Well, I wasn't going to stand for that, and they weren't going to tolerate me. After that meeting, they took every opportunity to berate me publicly and viciously—business meetings, deacons meetings, you name it. Moreover, that group had long given up on the notion that they would be able to control me if I ever became pastor. So they assembled a pulpit committee made up of forty of the most influential and wealthy members of the church, who were sure to support whatever choice they made. Then they found four other candidates for the position of senior pastor—most of them liberal, all of them seemingly very political.

From that point on, those seven men focused their efforts on disparaging me. It was as if I somehow stood in the way of their calling the man they wanted—even though they could fire me at any moment. They said horrible things—wining and dining church members to get them to turn against me. People would hug me one week and say, "I want you to know that you have my support," and then refuse to speak to me at all the next. It was devastating.

Likewise, members of the gang of seven would invite me to lunch with the intention of inducing me to leave. "Just go on vacation and don't come back," they would say. "We'll give you whatever you want." It made me angry that they would even suggest such a thing.

Repeatedly, I told them, "I didn't come to this church because of you. I came because God called me to come here. And I'll be happy to leave the minute God tells me to do so." I wasn't about to willfully disobey the Father because of them, no matter what they did or offered me. I knew that if I left, I'd assume the responsibility for doing so. But if I stood true to the Lord and they made the decision to fire me, they would bear the consequences of it.

Still, those men knew how to strike me where it would wound the deepest. During that time, I developed a friendship with a man whom I cared for as a brother in Christ. Later I learned that he was merely pretending to be my friend in order to get information for the group in an effort to undermine my authority. Thankfully, God revealed his true character and what he was trying to accomplish before he could do any real damage. But I was profoundly hurt that anyone would be so deceitful.

All of that worked together to make me feel like an outcast at the church. Almost all of the staff members turned against me. And as I would walk out on Sunday mornings, I knew that of the two or three thousand people in attendance, at least three hundred of them were actively, virulently against me. Even more painful was how intent they were on making it known that they couldn't stand me. They would walk up and down the halls of the church singing, "We will overcome," meaning, they would overcome *me*. I would just think, *God, what in the world can be done about this? How is this ever going to work out?*

If I stood true to the Lord and they made the decision to fire me, they would bear the consequences.

I thought that the only allies I had at the time were ten women who met regularly to pray for me. I found out later that another group of prayer-warriors would gather in a large room upstairs in the Atlanta Garden Center, which was owned by my friend Charles Bell. They would intercede with God on my behalf—asking Him to keep me strong and to glorify Himself though FBA. I was also grateful that when I got home at the end of the day, Annie and the children would gather around me and pray to the Father for me. Their support meant the world to me, and I praised God for it.

During that time, I also received repeated requests from an eighty-year-old retired nurse named Mrs. Sauls to come to her house for lunch. I didn't feel as if I had the time to visit her, but she was so persistent that I finally gave in. Thank God I did.

When I arrived, she said she had something she wanted to show me, and she led me up the stairs to a picture she had hung on a wall. It was a beautiful portrait of *Daniel in the Lions' Den*, a copy of the painting by Briton Rivière. It depicted the biblical story of the prophet Daniel, who had prayed to the God of Israel and was being punished for it by ungodly enemies who were jealous of the favor he had with King Darius (Dan. 6). The sentence he faced was death by lions.

Quietly, Mrs. Sauls said, "Son, look at that picture. I want you to tell me what you see." I described the scene as best I could. It showed the lions gathered behind Daniel, their mouths closed. There were bones on the floor—apparently the remnants of others who'd been sentenced to the same punishment. But Daniel appeared calm, peaceful, and amazingly unconcerned. He held his hands behind his back, and he looked up at the light that streamed in through the bars on the window of his cell. It was such a dignified stance.

She asked, "Is there anything else?"

I replied, "No, ma'am."

I have never forgotten what she said next—it was one of the wisest, most powerful sermons I'd ever heard. Mrs. Sauls put her arm around my waist and said, "Son, Daniel doesn't have his eyes on the lions. He has them on God."

It was as if Jesus Himself had wrapped His loving arms around me, filling me with strength and comfort. Nothing could have been more profoundly needed in my life at just that moment. She was saying, "Charles, don't look at your enemies. You just keep your focus on God. He's going to see you through this."

And it was completely true. As long as I kept my eyes on the Father, He gave me peace that surpassed my comprehension. And He continued to give me assurances of His plan through His Word and as I went before Him in prayer.

One Friday, about four o'clock in the afternoon, I was facedown, praying for the Lord's guidance and power. As usual, God spoke to my heart, "I'm going to make you the pastor of this church, just trust Me. Don't do a thing. Pray. Keep quiet. Don't say a word. Don't defend yourself. Just trust Me."

During another time of prayer, the Lord admonished me, "This is the way you are going to win this battle. See everything that happens to you as coming from Me. No matter what they say or do—see it as coming from Me, because I am in control."

It was exactly what I needed, especially with so many against me.

The whole situation reminded me of God's powerful provision to King Jehoshaphat and the nation of Judah, when they faced an impossible onslaught from three different armies—the Moabites, the Ammonites, and the Meunites. The Judahites had nothing with which to defend themselves, so Jehoshaphat cried out to God, "We are powerless before this great multitude who are coming against us; nor do we know what to do, but our eyes are on You" (2 Chron. 20:12).

God spoke to my heart, "Just trust Me. Don't do a thing. Pray. Keep quiet. Don't defend yourself. Just trust Me."

The Father responded with a heavenly declaration through His servant Jahaziel, "Do not fear or be dismayed because of this great multitude, for the battle is not yours but God's . . . You need not fight in this battle; station yourselves, stand and see the salvation of the LORD on your behalf" (2 Chron. 20:15, 17).

The same was true for me. The fight was not mine but God's. And the battleground—First Baptist Atlanta—was not theirs; it was *His*. The Father had more interest in taking back the church than I could ever comprehend because He was reconquering territory for the advancement of His Kingdom—for countless generations after me. Like King Jehoshaphat and the nation of Judah, I was simply a tool in His hand as He defended His rightful property. My place of combat was not at the pulpit or during business meetings, but stretched out before God in the prayer room.

Subsequently, every day I would go before the throne of grace, seek the Lord's face, and say, "Father, help me to go out to the pulpit full of Your Spirit and power." And every Sunday, the Lord empowered me to do just that. I preached as if nothing had been said against me all week. And each time that awesome principle was proved true: When you fight your battles on your knees, you most certainly win every time.

VICTORY IN JESUS

In October 1971, I went up to Bryan College in Dayton, Tennessee, to speak at a weeklong student revival. While I was gone, the gang of seven realized that as long as I was at the pulpit preaching, none of the other pastoral candidates would have an opportunity to speak to the congregation and, therefore, would have no possibility of winning the people over. It became increasingly clear that if they truly wanted another man to be considered for the position of senior pastor, they had to find a way to get me out of the pulpit so the other candidates could preach.

So while I was away, the seven-man executive committee, the deacons, and the forty-member pulpit committee voted to eliminate me as a candidate for the role of senior pastor of First Baptist Atlanta and called a business meeting for the Wednesday after I returned from Tennessee. I knew they didn't want me, but this was still a surprise. Apparently, they had come up with a plan to convince the congregation to reject me.

That Saturday, I found out part of their strategy. A friend called to inform me that a leaflet had been placed on every seat in the sanctuary, as well as every chair in the Sunday school classrooms and fellowship areas. The leaflets enumerated all the reasons I should not be called as pastor and why I should no longer be allowed to preach.

During the week while I was up at Bryan College, I had a great deal of free time to pray, and I took advantage of it. I felt a profound oneness with God that gave me great peace. However, as I tried to prepare the Sunday morning sermon, I had no ideas—not even a passage of Scripture to anchor the message to.

In the back of my mind, I knew it was going to take courage to enter that sanctuary with leaflets on the pews. Imagine having to walk in to *that* on a Sunday morning! I knew this would be my last opportunity to speak to the congregation prior to the upcoming Wednesday night business meeting, when a vote would be taken about whether or not to call me as their senior pastor. Still, nothing came—I had nothing to say.

That Sunday morning, I woke up and still had no message. I thought about it all the way on my thirty-minute commute to the church, but I still didn't even have a verse from God's Word to focus on. Before the Sunday morning service, I went to my study at the church and wrote out a simple outline, just in case. But then I thought, *No, I've trusted God all these years, and I'm not going to start relying on myself now.* After all, Jesus told the disciples, "Do not worry about how or what you are to speak in your defense, or what you are to say; for the Holy Spirit will teach you *in that very hour* what you ought to say" (Luke 12:11–12; emphasis added).

So I prayed, "Lord, this is Your message to Your people. Speak through me, Father. I trust You to teach me what to say."

When it was time for the service, I threw the outline in the trash and made my way to the sanctuary. After the choir finished, I walked up to the pulpit, let my Bible fall open, and looked to see where it had landed. Immediately my eyes fell on one of my favorite verses, Proverbs 3:5–6: "Trust in the LORD with all your heart and do not lean on your own understanding. In all your ways acknowledge Him, and He will make your paths straight."

So I prayed, "Lord, this is Your message to Your people. Speak through me, Father. I trust You to teach me what to say."

I smiled. No passage of Scripture could have been more perfect. And for the next forty-five minutes, I couldn't speak fast enough. It was as if a dam of the Holy Spirit's power had burst free, and God's words flowed out of me nonstop about how to find His will and obey it without fear.

I don't have any earthly idea what I said. All I know is that when I was done, I gave the invitation. The next thing you know, everyone was up on their feet and moving. It was the most amazing thing I had ever seen at a church service. It was like a bomb had gone off, the power of God sent people sprinting in two distinct directions. The first group of people rushed down the aisles toward the exits. But on their way out, they passed an even bigger crowd of people who were streaming toward the altar—some for salvation, some to rededicate their lives, some to be baptized, some to join the church, some simply to pray.

It was as if God had thrown down the gauntlet, and each person was making his or her allegiance known.

Understand, I had not said the first word about the battle against me—I never mentioned it the whole time it was raging. I didn't try to manipulate the situation, denounce my accusers, or anything of the sort. All I did was pray and preach the Word. And God did the rest.

Well, that next Wednesday afternoon, just a few hours before the business meeting, two trial lawyers and a seminary professor came to see me. Actually, it appeared they came to intimidate me. They explained in no uncertain terms that I could not be the pastor of FBA and that if I did not resign that night, I would never pastor another Southern Baptist Church again. They would make sure I was ruined forever.

I thought, *Father, what is this?* But at that moment, it was like God's Spirit showed me that if that group of seven were truly confident that the congregational vote for senior pastor would go their way, they wouldn't have to threaten me. What they didn't seem to know was that all of this was in God's hands. Not theirs and not mine.

It was like a bomb had gone off, the power of God sent people sprinting in two distinct directions.

The Lord was in control. I knew that God was the one Who had brought me to this place, and I wasn't about to walk away from His clear calling.

I said to those lawyers, "You're welcome to fire me, but God has not told me to resign. I came here out of obedience to Him, because of His will. So I'll only leave if He calls me to. No hard feelings. I have to make a decision I can live with, and so do you."

Then the seminary professor—a man who had supposedly been teaching pastors for years—said, "What is this will of God business? How could you possibly think you can know the will of God?" I knew him to be liberal in his theology and this certainly confirmed it. I tried to explain it to him, but he wasn't about to listen to me. Thankfully, after that, he and the two lawyers saw there would be no moving me, so they got up and left.

When the time came for the business meeting, I went into the sanctuary and sat in the corner under the balcony, where it was somewhat dark and I was out of sight. I did not want to influence the vote in any way. It was God's battle to fight. As for me, my assignment was clear: "Cease striving and know that I am God" (Ps. 46:10).

I kept my Bible open to Isaiah 54:17: " 'No weapon that is formed against you will prosper; and every tongue that accuses you in judgment you will condemn. This is the heritage of the servants of the LORD, and their vindication is from Me,' declares the LORD." I watched and prayed as people came into the sanctuary and took their places, and I thanked God for how He was directing them (Dan. 2:21).

I couldn't deny that the Father was moving in people's hearts. I had never seen so many at a church business meeting—at least two thousand people. Almost the whole church had showed up to hash it out.

When the chairman of the board of deacons informed the congregation they would be voting by secret ballot, a man stood up in the back and said, "No, we're not! Tonight this church is going to find out where everybody stands. I make a motion that we take standing votes on every measure." His motion passed and people throughout the church began clapping. Applauding is commonplace now, but at that time in the early 1970s at First Baptist Atlanta, it was absolutely unheard of.

Regardless of that setback, the chairman announced, "We the deacons recommend that we remove Charles Stanley as acting pastor and demote him to his original position as associate pastor." Then they tried every parliamentary procedure they could think of to get rid of me. Thankfully, Henry Robert III—the grandson of Brigadier General Henry Martyn Robert, who wrote *Robert's Rules of Order*— was present and stopped all of their mischief. It didn't matter what kind of stunts they tried to pull, he caught them every time.

But here was what amazed me the most. In that long, drawn-out discussion to get rid of me, not one person ever said anything negative about me. Not one word.

I kept thinking, *Okay, who's going to give them some reasons to reject me?* But the Father spoke to my spirit, "Every tongue that accuses you in judgment I have condemned." That is how protective God is. Instead of defaming me, they simply wrangled among themselves.

Eventually, a fellow in the back stood up and said, "I want to make a substitute motion. I move that we call Charles Stanley as senior pastor of First Baptist Church!" Someone seconded the motion. You can imagine the uproar that ensued.

Realizing that their power was slipping away, the gang of seven kept stalling the vote and tried to kill the motion. Finally, Mrs. Sauls stood up and said, "Mr. Chairman, I call for the question!"

They had no choice. That group of seven were not only forced to take the vote but also to count it publicly. After that, there was no denying it—65 percent of the church stood to call me as pastor. The gang of seven with all their wealth, influence, underhanded tactics, and legal counsel could not thwart God's will. The Father had done just as He promised. Truly, "He who believes in Him will not be disappointed" (1 Pet. 2:6).

IT'S NOT OVER UNTIL IT'S OVER

At that point in the meeting, someone suggested they call me to report the outcome of the vote and to formally invite me to accept the position of senior pastor. Since I'd sat in a back corner where it was somewhat dark, few people realized that I was present. Boy, were they embarrassed to discover that I'd been there the entire time, listening to everything they said about me!

I came forward and said, "I appreciate your confidence. I'll give you an answer in two weeks."

You would think that the matter would have ended there and that the congregational vote would be accepted. But the seven men were so angry that they called a deacons' meeting a week later, where they took turns venting their anger toward me. They never accused me of anything; they just tried to bully and humiliate me into walking away as Dr. McClain had done.

I didn't say a word. I knew I didn't have to.

I just thought of Jesus before Pilate. Matthew 27:14 said, "He did not answer him with regard to even a single charge." Our Savior didn't say anything because in three days the Lord God would make the ultimate statement by raising Him from the grave.

Likewise, I understood that I didn't have to say a thing because the Father had already passed His judgment through the congregation and had given me the privileged opportunity to be the new pastor of First Baptist Church. The Body of Christ had spoken. That was what I focused on as they berated me. And I will confess, every once in a while I'd grin at the thought of how God had gotten the victory.

I had been called to be the new senior pastor, and I was grateful. But their public outbursts made it obvious to me that they would by no means go quietly. I spent the next two weeks in prayer, asking God to show me the next step.

The people against me were still in leadership positions. So for three months—from October 1971 to January 1972—they would attend Sunday school at FBA and then go down the street to a medical building that had an auditorium to have their own services. On Wednesday nights, they would all gather for dinner at one end of the dining hall and spend their time criticizing me. Then they would leave before the service.

Of course, throughout that time, I was praying for God's wisdom. Jesus said, "If a house is divided against itself, that house will not be able to stand" (Mark 3:25). If FBA was to become healthy again, and if the church was going to be a positive witness of Christ in the world, the unity would have to be restored. Otherwise, the enemy would be successful in undermining its effectiveness. However, I had absolutely no idea how that would occur.

If FBA was to become healthy again, and if the church was going to be a positive witness of Christ in the world, the unity would have to be restored.

I didn't harbor any anger or bitterness toward the people against me. Actually, I was grieved because they were missing the joy and fulfillment of the abundant Christian life. More than anything, I wanted them to know all the blessings available to them. But they were absolutely unwilling to accept my authority as senior pastor, or even to listen to me. In the end, because of the destruction they were causing in the church, all I could do was pray, "Father, change them or remove them."

Eventually, the Lord made it clear that I would have to take hold of the situation—I could not allow it to continue. So I discussed the problem with the Sunday school superintendent, who was an old army colonel and a friend of mine. I told him, "I'm going to ask the church to give you and me full authority to appoint new leadership."

He replied, "I'm with you a hundred percent."

We made plans to have a business meeting a week from then, on that next Wednesday. And during the week that followed, I continued to pray about the situation, making sure I had God's mind on it and that this was the way we needed to go.

That next Wednesday morning, on the day of the business meeting, the Father spoke to me through Psalm 64:

Hear my voice, O God, in my complaint; Preserve my life from dread of the enemy . . . They devise injustices, saying, "We are ready with a well-conceived plot"; for the inward thought and the heart of a man are deep. But God will shoot at them with an arrow; suddenly they will be wounded. So they will make him stumble; their own tongue is against them; all who see them will shake the head. Then all men will fear, and they will declare the work of God, and will consider what He has done. The righteous man will be glad in the Lord and will take refuge in Him; and all the upright in heart will glory. (vv. 1, 6–10)

I had been somewhat fearful about how that business meeting would go, but it was as if the Lord etched verse 7 in my heart: "God will shoot at them with an arrow; suddenly they will be wounded."

And that is exactly what happened. During the meeting, as planned, I asked the congregation to assign the task of appointing all the deacons and church officers to the Sunday school superintendent and to me instead of going through the education committee. A deacon and friend of that group of seven stood and asked if he could say something.

I said, "That's fine."

Well, he came up on the platform and gave an awful speech about the damage I was doing to First Baptist Atlanta—how I was stealing the church and running him away. He got all worked up and even used profanity. Of course, I wasn't going to tolerate that.

I stood beside him and said, "We're not going to have that kind of language here. You need to calm down or sit down."

He scowled. "Stanley, if you don't watch what you're doing, you're going to get hurt." He then backhanded me in the jaw with his fist.

I didn't flinch. I just stood there. A woman stood and shouted, "How dare you hit my pastor!" Her husband—a big, strong fellow— jumped up and rushed toward the platform, as did another man—a seventy-year-old former boxer, with a brass-handled cane. The boxer yelled, "You're not going to hit my pastor!" as he waved his cane in the air like a sword. I thought he was going to do some real damage! But they grabbed the man who'd hit me and hauled him out.

My son, Andy, who was thirteen at the time, tried to jump over the pew and get to me, but a deacon friend of mine grabbed him and held him back. He said, "Andy, it's okay. God just won this whole battle." And he was right. That man had identified himself and all the people with him as a group who could not control themselves and who were absolutely unworthy of leadership. In that moment, the Lord had shot them with an arrow and they were all wounded.

It took a while to restore order to the meeting, but soon the motion passed and the superintendent and I began to make plans to rebuild the leadership of the church.

However, as I drove to church that next Sunday, I had a restlessness in my spirit. That morning, God had spoken to me through Exodus

14:13–14: "Do not fear! Stand by and see the salvation of the LORD which He will accomplish for you today; for the Egyptians whom you have seen today, you will never see them again forever. The LORD will fight for you while you keep silent." So I was sure *something* was going to happen, though I had no idea what.

At that point, FBA was broadcasting on one Atlanta TV station in black and white. So when I got to the

> *"The LORD will fight for you while you keep silent."*

church, I contacted the cameramen and said, "Be on the alert today. If I give you a signal, turn the cameras off."

I am so glad I did. Right after we began singing the first hymn in the service, a man—who was on the *hospitality* committee, if you can believe it—came rushing up to the platform, pushed the minister of music, John Glover, out of the way, grabbed the microphone, and shouted, "Today, you haven't come to hear a sermon. You've come to witness a funeral."

I immediately signaled to the cameramen to cut the live feed and get us off the air, which they did. Three college students sitting in the congregation stood up and resumed the hymn, "Onward, Christian Soldiers," trying their best to drown out the man on the platform, who was in the middle of a tirade. Other church members caught on quickly, standing and singing as loudly as they could. They sang him down and kept singing until he'd been successfully escorted from the sanctuary.

Then next thing you know, the police were there. Apparently, a lady had been watching the service on television, saw the man rush the platform, heard what he said about a funeral, and then watched in horror as the program went off the air. She immediately called the authorities and said, "There's a black-bearded hippie taking over the First Baptist Church of Atlanta!" Remember, this was the early 1970s, when there were many protest marches and demonstrations—especially in the heart of Atlanta. Apparently, she thought FBA had been taken hostage by political or social activists.

But just the opposite was true. Finally, FBA was truly shaking free of the stranglehold that held it for so long. Over the next few days, thirty-eight of the sixty-five deacons, all of the Women's Missionary Union, thirty-five of the forty-eight choir members, half the Sunday school workers, and all but two of the staff resigned. The final blow was to threaten the television station that they would interrupt every worship service until the station took FBA off the air. The station could not afford such disruptions, so they ended their contract with us.

But then that was it. It was over.

In one fell swoop, that group of seven and all of their supporters were gone.

As you can imagine, all of this left the church somewhat crippled for leadership and broken internally. But I didn't despair. Instead, I understood that this is the principle that Jesus talks about in John 15:2: "Every branch in Me that does not bear fruit, He takes away; and every branch that bears fruit, He prunes it so that it may bear more fruit." As I said previously, my ultimate concern was the health of the church and its effectiveness in the world as an envoy of God's awesome message of salvation. Even though we had some difficult days ahead rebuilding what had been torn apart, I was confident the church would come back stronger and better than ever. The Lord had not brought us this far to do any less.

And the truth of the matter is that when all those people finally left, it was as if a heaviness lifted from the church. The ominous storm clouds hovering over the horizon that I'd seen in the vision from God were finally gone. It felt like it was morning again at First Baptist Atlanta—like Malachi 4:2 promised, "The sun of righteousness will rise with healing in its wings." In the light of the rising sun of God's grace, we could see the problems more clearly—especially the ones so long hidden by darkness—and therefore it was easier to confront and fix them (Matt. 10:26). I was filled with

Even though we had some difficult days ahead, I was confident the church would come back stronger than ever.

renewed boldness for the task and confidence in the Father's strength. And the congregation had a party to celebrate that the long war for the soul of the church was finally over.

GROWING PAINS

After the horrible battle the church had endured, the members were very motivated to serve God and move forward. It was like when Nehemiah asked the people to rebuild the walls of Jerusalem: "The people had a mind to work" (Neh. 4:6). I would announce from the pulpit that we had a need—such as choir members or Sunday school teachers—and invariably people would volunteer, eager for a way to serve.

It was an exciting time, and FBA grew immensely. People were accepting Jesus Christ as their Savior and growing spiritually. The church was branching out into new areas—such as starting the *Life of Christ Pageant* in 1977, which would later be called the *Atlanta Passion Play*. Likewise, in December 1979, we had our First World Missions Conference and began the Faith Promise program—challenging our members to give beyond their tithes to support FBA missionaries.

We could see God's hand guiding the progress and growth of FBA through all of it.

In fact, one year to the day that the gang of seven bullied that Atlanta station to take us off the air, we began broadcasting again— this time calling the program *The Chapel Hour* and airing on two stations that broadcast in color: WXIA-TV 11 and WANX 46. In addition, WGST 920 radio added us to their schedule. Those stations covered more than Atlanta—they reached into other areas of Georgia and even transmitted to parts of the Caribbean. So our influence was expanding, which thrilled me to no end. God had laid a burden on my heart to get the gospel beyond the four walls of the church. I prayed, "Lord, I want it to go as far as You want it to go. That's up to You. I'm going to work diligently and I'm going to trust You to have free reign in this ministry."

That was 1973. I used to look out the window of my study at the Elks Lodge building at 736 Peachtree Street. I would say, "Lord, we need room to grow, and I believe we could use that building more profitably than they can." That went on for six months. One day, the Elks administrator was talking to one of my staff members and asked, "By the way, would you all be interested in this building?" God had opened the door. So by 1974, we had purchased the Elks Lodge building and put our High School Ministry over there.

It was incredible. We kept expanding—buying more properties— and the people kept coming. By Super Sunday in 1975, we had an attendance of five thousand in church. On February 13, 1977, we began to have two worship services on Sundays instead of just one to accommodate all the people.

God had ushered us into a period of astounding growth and fruitfulness. Of course, as you can imagine, this also led to growing pains.

We struggled with where to put all the people we were reaching—they were joining faster than we could buy property. But that was a wonderful problem to have, and we saw that not every battle is negative. Sometimes we are simply hindered by our own limitations and must overcome them in the same way we would conquer any other obstacle or enemy—on our knees in prayer.

ON TRACK FOR BLESSINGS

In early 1981, a building right across the street from the church belonging to Capital Cadillac became available for sale. The property included that whole block. We had already purchased the two blocks beyond that building, so it would add continuity to the church grounds.

The problem was that the property was selling for $2,850,000 and the money was due in just six weeks—on Monday, March 2, at noon. On all our previous property purchases we had never borrowed money; rather, we trusted God to work out His will. However, we'd never raised such an enormous *God had ushered us into a period of astounding growth and fruitfulness.* amount. It seemed impossible, of course. But I knew that "with God all things are possible" (Matt. 19:26), so I took the opportunity to the congregation on January 11. They voted to purchase the building and began to give generously, as they always had.

Unfortunately, it was not enough. Just eight days before the deadline, on Sunday, February 22, we had raised only $125,000—not even 5 percent of the total amount needed. Even worse, it had gotten out to the press that we were trying to buy that building without going into debt. Major television stations and newspapers were tracking our progress. It seemed as if the whole world was about to see us fail.

A couple of my deacons were so afraid of humiliation that they suggested going down to the bank and arranging a loan just in case we couldn't raise the money. But I made it crystal clear: We were not going to borrow one copper penny.

That morning, God laid it on my heart to preach a message titled "Who Then Is Willing?" about 1 Chronicles 28 and 29, when David made preparations for building the Temple. If you recall, the Lord told David that because he had shed blood and been a man of war, he could not have the honor of constructing His habitation. Instead, David's son, Solomon, would be the one to raise the Temple. But as a concession, because of His loving-kindness, God allowed David to collect the materials needed.

So David went before Israel and asked, "Who then is willing to consecrate himself this day to the Lord?" (1 Chron. 29:5). I like the original Hebrew wording, which says, "Who then is willing this day to come with full hands before the Lord?" That is, who is willing to bring God all that he or she has in order to build Him a temple and finish the work that He has planned for us to accomplish?

David wanted the rest of Israel to share in the blessing of seeing the Temple constructed and having a part in it. You see, the needs God makes us aware of are like tracks through which He sends our blessings. We get on board with Him by doing as He asks, and that creates the path by which we see His provision and join in His victory.

Jesus said it like this: "Give, and it will be given to you. They will pour into your lap a good measure—pressed down, shaken together, and running over. For by your standard of measure it will be measured to you in return" (Luke 6:38).

David wanted that for the Israelites—he wanted them to experience the overflowing joy of seeing God do a mighty work through them. But first, it would require them to trust the Father more than their own resources and make the sacrifices He directed. If they clung to their worldly wealth and sources of security instead of to Him, they would miss the blessing.

When we get on board with God by doing as He asks, that creates the path by which we see His provision and join in His victory.

I then showed the congregation three long strands of hair and said, "So what is God requiring of us? The Lord is calling us to trust Him—to burn every bridge, break every tie, cut every single hair of any possibility of retreating or depending upon anything but God." With that, I cut the strands of hair.

The same principle applies today. When God calls us to seemingly impossible tasks beyond our resources, we cannot cling to our meager wealth, understanding, talents, abilities, or worldly connections. We must pour them out as an offering and embrace those great assignments out of obedience to Him. Then we will see Him supernaturally supply all that we're lacking.

That is what happened with the Capital Cadillac building. When I finished the message at the early service, a young couple came forward and said, "God told us to give you this jewelry. It is the only valuable thing we own." It was the young woman's wedding ring. Well, I couldn't accept that! I insisted she take it back. But they stressed that the Lord had moved them to give it, and they did not want to disobey Him.

I was touched, so much so that I talked about this young couple's sacrifice during the second service. Apparently, the rest of the congregation was affected, too. When I gave the invitation, people came from every corner of the sanctuary to the altar, laying down money, jewelry, keys to cars, all manner of valuables, offerings, and sacrifices. It was astounding—a spiritual revival had begun.

And it continued throughout the week. People gave furniture, guns, boats, campers, antiques, and every kind of valuable you can imagine. Students at the church held car washes and bake sales. People just wanted to give whatever they could, coming with full hands before the Lord.

When God calls us to seemingly impossible tasks beyond our resources, He will supernaturally supply all that we're lacking.

One man even came to my office and said, "My wife and I were going to build a new house, but God told us to give that money to the church instead so you can buy the Cadillac building. We can build our house next year." And then he gave me a check for $500,000.

I felt my conviction growing. Annie and I had already sold our car and travel trailer and had given all the money toward purchasing the building. But I felt as if the Lord was asking me to relinquish something even more valuable and meaningful to me. As I prayed about what I could sell, God pinpointed what He wanted me to turn over to Him—my cameras. That was painful because, as I've said, I love photography. It's a hobby that allows me to exalt the Father and also helps me to relax. Surely, the Lord didn't want me to give those cameras up, did He? After all, they weren't worth that much. Any offering that resulted from them would be relatively minor compared to the sacrifices others were making.

But that wasn't the point, and I knew it. This was about whether my heart was tied up in those cameras or if it belonged completely to God. And there was only one choice I could really live with. So

I gathered all my equipment and handed it over to my friend King Grant, who bought and sold used gear at his business, KEH Camera Brokers.

I knew that people throughout the congregation were making the same choices and cleansing their hearts before the Lord. They were giving sacrificially, confessing their sins, and getting right with each other. It was amazing to see the broken relationships that were mended and the families that were made stronger.

Did we make our goal? Yes. God certainly got us to where we needed to be and we were able to purchase the Capital Cadillac building debt free. But even more important, that experience revitalized the church and sent a shot of Holy Spirit adrenaline through the Body of Christ in a way that could never be mimicked by man-made methods. We had been growing quickly, but we had yet to see the kind of growth the Lord intended for FBA.

EXCEEDINGLY, ABUNDANTLY, ABOVE AND BEYOND

Well, we'd seen that God's timing and provision were perfect, but we were about to experience that His battle plans are without compare even when they seem totally unreasonable. You see, by 1985, FBA owned seventeen acres of land and thirteen buildings. This provided classroom space, office areas, parking, and overflow rooms for worship. As we continued to expand in our membership throughout the 1980s and early '90s, however, we quickly realized it still wasn't enough. We filled the sanctuary and foyer to overflowing, with chairs lined up and down both aisles for every service. Unfortunately, this violated building codes, and the Atlanta fire marshal told us that we could not continue to operate in that manner. In fact, he came back and told us that three times. So we faced a real dilemma. It looked as if we would have to turn people away—which went against everything we were working toward. Surely, that was not an option.

After a great deal of discussion, it seemed that the best plan was for me to preach three services on Sunday mornings instead of two. This would be very difficult physically—two sermons in a row was demanding enough. I had tried preaching three messages in a row before—and lasted only ten weeks. But now we had no choice, so I trusted that God would give me the energy I needed.

Thankfully, to lighten my load, Andy—who had been on staff for several years at that point—agreed to take Sunday nights. So we decided that by August 1991, we would expand to three services and worked toward that goal—even enlisting a whole new leadership team to minister to people who came to the third service.

That fall, as was our usual practice, the staff and I went on a two-day prayer retreat. As we interceded on behalf of the church, we became more and more uneasy with the plans we'd made. Our conversation somehow led us to the early church and to the Council of Jerusalem, which I discussed earlier in this chapter. As you may recall, the church had a dilemma about the behavioral and dietary guidelines they were giving the Gentiles. They didn't want to pile unrealistic or needless requirements upon these new Christians, and so they discussed how best to teach them.

One of my staff members felt led to read Acts 15:28 out loud: "It seemed good to the Holy Spirit and to us to lay upon you no greater burden than these essentials." That verse hit home with me and the rest of the group. We immediately began to ask the Holy Spirit to make His will known to us—convinced that what we'd been planning was not actually God's desire for us.

We continued to intercede throughout the remainder of our retreat. But by the time it ended, only one thing was truly clear—we were not supposed to start that third Sunday worship service.

When we got home, I began to watch for God's activity—not just within the church but also throughout downtown Atlanta. It was then I realized that businesses were buying up properties and the area was becoming increasingly congested. Other churches downtown were stagnating and dying because they were landlocked. And if FBA stayed in that location, I was sure the same would happen to us.

So one day during a staff meeting, I put a big map on a wall and I said, "One of these days, we're going to have to think about moving, because we've run out of options here." Understand, this was a radical thing for me to say. First Baptist had been in the heart of Atlanta since 1848—before the first shot of the Civil War had been fired. It had been on that particular Peachtree Street lot since 1930. To many in the congregation, being downtown was a nonnegotiable part of the church's identity and heritage. Likewise, the beautiful First Baptist building itself, which was constructed to resemble the historic and stately St. Martin-in-the-Fields Anglican church in London, held a special place in people's hearts.

It seemed outlandish to even consider moving. After all, we owned so much property downtown. Where would we find a comparable location to house us? How could we transport such a large operation across town? And how would we motivate our people to go with us? So we had a choice—cling to the past or move forward with God. I pointed to a spot on the northeastern rim of I-285 and said, "If I could go anywhere, here's where I'd go." I didn't know anything about that area, but for some reason I felt that was where the Lord was directing us to look.

Just two months later, we found that right in the center of where

I'd pointed was where Avon's southeastern distribution branch had been headquartered—and where FBA is now located, at 4400 North Peachtree Road in Dunwoody. As I walked through the building, looking at all the machinery, conveyor belts, and loading docks, it was so different from what we had that I thought the people would never go for it. But in that moment, it was like the Lord spoke to my heart, "They've been making soap in this building and cleansing people physically for years. But now I'm going to work through you here to clean them up spiritually." So as counterintuitive as it seemed from a human standpoint, if moving here was the Father's choice, it would be mine as well.

On October 16, 1988, the congregation of FBA voted to buy the Avon property as the new church site, and by April 19, 1992, we had our first morning service in the Dunwoody location. Thankfully, we were able to sell the downtown properties for far more than what we'd paid for them—enough money that we were not only able to purchase and completely renovate the new building but also were left with a significant

If moving here was the Father's choice, it would be mine as well.

financial reserve for future expansion. Better location, more land, bigger building, room to grow, a greater store of resources, and everyone would be under one roof—not thirteen separate properties. It was exceedingly, abundantly, above and beyond all we could have asked or imagined (Eph. 3:20–21). Only God could have worked all that out.

DENOMINATIONAL BATTLES

Of course, every battle we endure in our lives prepares us for those ahead. And those early years of opposition at FBA and struggles for the future of the church were practice for what I was about to face, which was a war for the soul of the Southern Baptist Convention.

The year was 1984 and the SBC had been facing a terrible conflict between liberals and conservatives concerning the Word of God. Conservatives like myself maintained that the Bible is the inerrant, infallible, eternal Word of the living God. That is, it is without error, and when we read Scripture and allow the Holy Spirit to apply it to our lives, it transforms us supernaturally.

Hebrews 4:12 tells us, "The word of God is living and active and sharper than any two-edged sword, and piercing as far as the division of soul and spirit, of both joints and marrow, and able to judge the thoughts and intentions of the heart." In other words, through Scripture, the Holy Spirit speaks to the deepest parts of our soul—healing our wounds, convicting us of sin, encouraging us, and revealing truth that we could not know otherwise. This is the inherent power of God's Word. Through it, the Lord moves us to change beyond our own ability to do so. And it doesn't matter who we are, where we come from, or how we grew up, because the Holy Spirit Himself explains it to us in a way we can understand (Ps. 19:7).

In fact, the Word of God is so powerful that when Ezra the priest stood and read it aloud, the people of Israel were brought tears of repentance and revival broke out (Neh. 8:1–12). Ezra needed no theatrics or rhetorical strategies; he didn't tailor his message to his audience or have brilliant showmanship. He just read Scripture. And through it, the Lord got hold of the nation and set it back on the right track.

Biblical conservatives have a very high view of the Bible. And, of course, we have a good reason for it. Jesus, the Son of God— also called the Word of God (John 1:1)—often quoted or referenced Scripture when He taught. In fact, He said, "Everyone who hears these words of Mine and acts on them, may be compared to a wise man who built his house on the rock. And the rain fell, and the floods came, and the winds blew and slammed against that house; and yet it did not fall, for it had been founded on the rock" (Matt. 7:24–25).

This is because what we have in the Bible are the very words and thoughts of God Himself. It's not "just another book" or even a "great book," because it is completely transcendent and unlike any other volume that's ever been published. It is the written record of the Lord's unfolding revelation of His ways, character, and nature through the spoken word, in history, and ultimately through the coming of Jesus Christ into the world. So Scripture is the main way we know the Father, and it's the agent the Lord works through to conform us to His character, transform us into His likeness, and renew our minds, so that we

What we have in the Bible are the very words and thoughts of God Himself.

"may prove what the will of God is, that which is good and acceptable and perfect" (Rom. 12:2).

Conversely, liberals and moderates don't teach this, and at the time, they were the ones holding important positions in Southern Baptist colleges and seminaries—shaping the next generation of pastors, ministers, and missionaries. Instead of challenging upcoming leaders to approach the future with the courage, faith, and reverence of Abraham, David, and Daniel, they were instructing them to pick and choose the relevant portions of Scripture and make the gospel more palatable. As you can imagine, this was a serious problem. Inherently, this put the responsibility on the individual to decide what was important to grow his congregation, rather than allowing the Lord to lead, empower, convict, and transform.

Well, something had to be done about it, and other conservative leaders asked me to step up and run for president of the SBC. But I had absolutely no interest in public office, and I didn't think I would make a very good parliamentarian. As I recounted previously, during the '80s, FBA was growing by leaps and bounds and we were wrestling with where to put everyone. I had enough on my plate without taking on anything else.

Also, my godly friend Dr. Ed Young was pastor of Second Baptist in Houston, Texas, and I thought he could do a fantastic job as president. I was positive he'd have a better chance at being elected than I would. So I fasted and prayed about it and remained convinced it was not something I should commit to.

That year, the convention began on June 12 and met in Kansas City, Missouri. The night before the election, I met with a group of pastors to pray because we were still unsure who the conservative candidate would be. They agreed with me that Dr. Young should be our choice for president.

However, Bertha Smith, who had been a missionary to China and Taiwan for more than forty years, said to me, "Charles, get down on your knees right now and repent! You know that God's called you to be the president—so get down there and repent right now." Miss Bertha was eighty-four years old and was one of the most spirit-filled ladies you could wish to meet, so I wasn't about to argue with her. I got on my knees and did just what she told me. But I still went away from that meeting believing the burden was off my shoulders. When

I got back to the room and told Annie what had happened, she said, "Well, thank God that's all settled."

So the next day—the day of the election—I woke up, got ready as usual, and walked to the door with the intention of heading out to the floor of the convention. But when I reached for the doorknob, the Spirit of God stopped me in my tracks. The Father said to me, "Don't put your hand on that doorknob until you're willing to do what I ask."

I fell on my face at the end of the bed and wept. I knew that I was at one of those major crossroads of life—much like the one I faced when God called me to FBA. The Lord was saying, "Here is your choice: You can do as I tell you and discover all the amazing things I desire to accomplish through you, or you can disobey Me and spend the rest of your life wondering what I could have done if you had submitted to My plan."

I knew what I had to do—I had to obey. And I realized that no matter what, the Lord would be with me. After all, hadn't I asserted that the Word of God was true, without error, living, active, and powerful? And didn't it say, "The LORD is the one who goes ahead of you; He will be with you. He will not fail you or forsake you. Do not fear or be dismayed" (Deut. 31:8)? I couldn't possibly assert that I believed in the infallibility and reliability of Scripture and then not obey whatever the Father commanded me. The choice was crystal clear: Either I really believed that the biblical record of God's miraculous provision to the saints of old was absolutely true and would prove it by staking my life on it (Rom. 15:4), or I didn't and by default would show that my opponents were right. I trust you know what I chose.

I prayed, "Father, if that's what You want, I am willing to obey. I don't want to miss Your best for my life. So no matter how difficult this becomes, my answer to You is 'Yes!' " I was certain that the battle ahead would be excruciating and greater than any I'd ever faced before. But I was also confident that "victory belongs to the Lord" (Pr. 21:31) and that He wouldn't have brought me this far if He didn't have a good purpose for it.

Well, when I finally got down to the convention where the other pastors were, I discovered that they had prayed all night and that the Father had stopped Dr. Young from moving forward with the nomination. Ed felt deeply that the Lord was telling him, "No." So I stepped up and braced myself for the battles ahead.

Almost immediately, I was asked by the press what I thought of my chances. I just said, "If I win, I win. And if I lose, I win because my responsibility is to obey God and leave the results to Him. Winning is doing what He told me to do, so I win either way." And it was true. It didn't matter to me how the election turned out—I just wanted whatever the Father wanted.

"Father, I am willing to obey. I don't want to miss Your best for my life."

Apparently the Lord wanted me to be president of the SBC because I was elected with 52.18 percent of the vote over the moderate and independent candidates. In 1985, I ran again at the convention in Dallas, which had the largest number of messengers in SBC history—45,519 were in attendance. Again, I won the nomination, this time with 55.3 percent of the vote.

And as expected, it turned out to be an exceedingly contentious season. But thankfully, it was also a turning point for the SBC. My election infuriated the opposition and ultimately revealed many of the underlying problems that had existed in the convention for a long time but had either been ignored or denied. I had never seen anything like it—and considering what I'd faced at FBA, that's saying a great deal.

All the liberal and moderate political forces of the Southern Baptist Convention were against me, which included seminary presidents and state convention newspapers. It was a pure war zone, and I was constantly under attack from every side.

Unexpectedly, however, throughout that time I had an unusual sense of tranquility—"the peace of God, which surpasses all comprehension" (Phil. 4:7). I knew I was in the center of His will, so I never felt anxious or angry even when the conflicts were at their very worst. Instead, I clung to three verses the Father gave me, and they garrisoned my heart about like a fortress:

- "The steadfast of mind You will keep in perfect peace, because he trusts in You" (Isa. 26:3).
- "I have put My words in your mouth and have covered you with the shadow of My hand" (Isa. 51:16).
- "Take no thought for your life, what ye shall eat, or what ye shall drink; nor yet for your body, what ye shall put on. Is not the life more than meat, and the body than raiment? . . . But seek ye first the kingdom of God, and his righteousness; and all these things shall be added unto you" (Matt. 6:25, 33, KJV).

Regardless of what anyone said or did, those verses were my anchor during the storms. That's not to say it wasn't painful; it often was. We began the process of cleaning up the SBC and bringing in conservative leaders to replace those who didn't view Scripture as the inerrant Word of God. And there was nothing easy about that. Sadly, what grieved me most during that time was the pastors who pledged to support conservative principles in private and then refused to stand for them in public out of fear of what their friends would think.

But thankfully, the Lord never wavered, and I never lost sight of His unfailing faithfulness to me. Every step of the way, I was confident He was in control. And time after time, He showed that He certainly was.

Did I handle everything perfectly during that time? Of course not. Was everything set right during those two years of my presidency? No. Nor did I expect it all to be. But during that season, the Southern Baptist Convention grew and made important strides in the home and international mission fields. Likewise, we took crucial steps in restoring the SBC and its colleges and seminaries to what they should have been doing—teaching the next generation that every servant of God who stands in the pulpit has a responsibility to preach in the power of the Holy Spirit and to proclaim the truth from Scripture.

THE PATH TO VICTORY

The point is, God is going to call you to fight some battles in your life. Some will be very difficult and disheartening because other people will be involved. The Lord will call you to be faithful to Him when others stand in opposition to you because they are not living by the same values, standards, or calling you are. At other times, the war will be against your own limitations in order to stretch your faith.

The most important thing to remember whenever you face a battle is that there can be only one Commander in Chief.

The most important thing to remember whenever you face a battle is that there can be only one Commander in Chief, and if you want to be victorious, that role can be filled only by God. You don't have to take the lead or manipulate your circumstances. On the contrary, your combat strategy must begin and end with confidence that the Lord is in control of your situation and that He is actively resolving it for you when you obey Him.

Therefore, in order to honor God and stay on the path to victory, here are the seven principles that will support you as you face the conflicts before you.

FIRST, ALWAYS FIGHT YOUR BATTLES ON YOUR KNEES. When you do, you'll win every time. Friend, don't engage your opponents in public, and don't ever attempt to do combat in your own strength. Instead, realize that "our struggle is not against flesh and blood, but against the rulers, against the powers, against the world forces of this darkness, against the spiritual forces of wickedness in the heavenly places" (Eph. 6:12). The Lord, your Defender, is working in indescribable ways to deliver you in the unseen and knows the route to success better than you can possibly imagine. This is why whenever you fight your battles on your knees, you put yourself in the perfect posture to triumph. So trust the Father to lead you through your time with Him in prayer.

SECOND, DECIDE BEFOREHAND THAT YOU'RE GOING TO OBEY GOD, REGARDLESS OF WHAT HAPPENS. You cannot wait until you're in the midst of a conflict to make this decision, because when the enemy is firing at you, you are more likely to react in your flesh than in a way that honors the Lord. So before a battle even begins, be the kind of person who obeys God and puts the principles of His Word into practice (Ps. 119:112; James 1:22). This alone will help keep you before the throne of grace and in the center of His will.

THIRD, FIND YOUR STRENGTH IN GOD. In other words, when you see problems lined up against you, don't measure them against your limited power, wisdom, and resources. Instead, judge them in terms of what the Lord can do. As the prophet Jeremiah proclaimed, "Lord God! Behold, You have made the heavens and the earth by Your great power and by Your outstretched arm! Nothing is too difficult for You!" (Jer. 32:17). Your heavenly Father is all-powerful, full of wisdom, and unconditionally loving. Not only can He defend you, but when you are walking in His will, He promises He will most certainly be your Rock, Deliverer, Stronghold, and Shield (Ps. 18:2).

Fourth, refuse to run away. No matter how bad things get or how tempted you are to quit, never make a move until the Lord Himself directs you to (Gal. 6:9; Heb. 10:35–36). You have no idea what God wants to do through you right where you are. And if you turn away from Him when the struggle is at its worst, you may never see the triumph or the blessings the Father has for you beyond the battle. As James 1:12 promises, "Blessed is a man who perseveres under trial; for once he has been approved, he will receive the crown of life which the Lord has promised to those who love Him." And certainly, you don't want to miss that.

Fifth, guard your lips. We can do more damage with our words than we can possibly imagine. In fact, James 3:5 says, "The tongue is a small part of the body, and yet it boasts of great things. See how great a forest is set aflame by such a small fire!" Through all of my battles, I made sure not to talk about those who opposed me, and I never defended myself, but I always kept the focus on what God said in His Word. Why? Because godly silence is very powerful. And if you don't say anything, you'll never have anything to take back. As Ecclesiastes 10:12 reminds us, "Words from the mouth of a wise man are gracious, while the lips of a fool consume him."

SIXTH, BE ALERT TO GROWING WEARY. When the battle grows long and people are criticizing you, you will become spiritually and emotionally exhausted. That is a dangerous place to be because you become more vulnerable to temptation and more likely to make bad decisions. Instead, observe the H.A.L.T. principle. When you start getting too Hungry, Angry, Lonely, or Tired, take it as a cue that it's time to stop, seek God, refuel, and refocus.

FINALLY, TO STAY ON THE PATH TO VICTORY, YOU MUST SEE EV-ERYTHING THAT HAPPENS AS COMING FROM GOD HIMSELF. This is one of the most important principles you can learn. It will protect you from anger, bitterness, and unforgiveness. It will also turn every trial you experience into a bridge to a deeper relationship with the Father. Why? Because it reminds you that "God causes all things to work together for good to those who love God, to those who are called according to His purpose" (Rom. 8:28).

Instead of seeing the battles against you as a curse, you understand that your loving heavenly Father has planned some special blessing for you through them—that the difficulties you face are ultimately opportunities that will bring you good and will give Him glory. Likewise, knowing that He has permitted the troubles in your life for your benefit makes it easier to forgive those who hurt you and helps you endure as long as the battle rages.

So whenever you face a battle, ask, "God, what is Your goal for allowing this to happen in my life?" Before you know it, you will be praising Him for the very skirmishes that once caused you such grief.

Friend, you can make it through the battles and conflicts you're facing. Not only that, but you can "overwhelmingly conquer through Him who loved" you (Rom. 8:37). You do so by keeping your eyes on the Lord, staying silent, and letting Him defend you. So don't lose heart and do not fear. Instead, "Stand by and see the salvation of the LORD which He will accomplish for you" (Ex. 14:13).

Long ago, I read this quotation, and it has stayed with me throughout the years: "When someone has the conviction that he or she is doing the work God gave him or her to do, there is a zeal and a courage in his or her soul that all the forces of this world cannot destroy."

That is so true. When you know you are doing the Lord's work in His timing and in His way, there is a confident boldness that keeps you going no matter what obstacles arise. He becomes your strength, your peace, and your assurance regardless of how everything looks around you.

So take heart, friend. All is not lost. Continue to fight your battles on your knees, stay in the center of His will, and trust Him. Because if you do, you'll find that He will lead you to greater victories than you've ever imagined.

✳

MY DAD, MY HERO
by Andy Stanley

I was thirteen when I learned the meaning of the phrase "Actions speak louder than words." My dad was an associate pastor at First Baptist Church of Atlanta when the senior pastor resigned under pressure from the board of deacons. While a search was conducted for a fitting replacement, my father was asked to "fill the pulpit." That's church talk for "preach on Sundays."

Well, fill it he did. And not only did he fill the pulpit, he started filling the pews as well. Young families started returning to the church in record numbers. The youth ministry began to grow. Volunteering was at an all-time high. Everybody was excited about the new energy that radiated from this historic downtown church.

Well, almost everybody.

As is the case in too many churches, there was a group of men and women who had been around longer than everybody else and felt as if the church somehow belonged to them. After all, it was their money that paid for most of the new chapel. And apart from their influence, the city may have never allowed the church to build the gymnasium. These people chaired all the key committees, including the committee on committees that determined who served on the committees. They were the *they* of First Baptist Atlanta. And *they* did not appreciate my dad's sudden popularity or the influence it gave him with the membership.

To make matters worse, there was a grassroots movement

afoot to elect my dad as senior pastor. And why not? He
was a phenomenal communicator. He demonstrated great
leadership ability. And he had a vision for the church. What
more could a congregation ask for? Depends on who you
were asking.

The power people thought he was too young (he was
forty), too evangelistic (he invited people to come forward
at the end of services), and too mystical. By "mystical"
they meant that he preached openly about a personal relationship with God. He also had the nerve to challenge the
congregation to pray for God's will concerning the future of
the church. Now *that* was a real problem. Before that time
the power people simply got together and decided the future
of the church; the notion of seeking God's will on the matter
was completely foreign to them.

Bottom line, *they* knew they would not be able to control
Dad. So they had but one choice: get rid of him. At first
they asked nicely for him to step down. Then they bribed
him. Eventually the bribes turned to threats. Not made-
for-primetime, CNN Presents–type threats. *They* were more
subtle than that. Essentially, they assured my father that if
he would leave quietly, there would certainly be a plethora
of other ministry opportunities open to him at other Baptist
churches. But if he insisted on staying and causing trouble,
he might never work in another Baptist church again. They
could ruin him—or so they claimed.

My dad's response to all of this marked me for life. The
way he saw it, God had brought him to that place. And when
God told him to leave, he would load us all up in the Grand

✳

Safari station wagon and we would go. There were times
when he asked God for permission to leave, but he always
received the same answer: *Stay where you are. Keep doing what
you are doing.* Dad was very up front with the group that
wanted him gone. He assured them that if the congregation
voted him out, he would leave quietly. That would be his
assurance that God had another ministry assignment for him
elsewhere.

Well, things continued to heat up. The power brokers
started taking members of the congregation to dinner. People
started taking sides. Nasty things were said, anonymous
letters written and distributed. It was church politics at their
worst. Yet in spite of all that, the church continued to grow
and prosper.

Then the church meeting to end all church meetings took
place.

It was about two weeks before the church was scheduled
to come together and vote on whether or not to allow my dad
to continue in his role as associate pastor. I was sitting about
six rows back on the right during our regular Wednesday
evening service. The program was just beginning when
one of the deacons walked up to the pulpit to make an announcement. Deacon Myers was part of the crew committed
to my dad's speedy departure.

Once "Brother" Myers finished his brief announcement,
he began sharing some of his personal feelings about the
brewing controversy. The longer he talked, the more angry
and animated he became. Then, to everyone's horror, he used

the word "damn." I'll never forget sitting in a Baptist church in 1972 and hearing a deacon say "damn" from the behind the pulpit. My dad immediately stood, walked up beside Deacon Myers, and said, "Now, you need to watch your language."

Before my dad could finish his sentence, the deacon raised a fist toward my dad's face and said, "No, you'd better watch *yourself*, or you might get punched!"

Frozen in my memory is the still picture of Deacon Myer's clenched fist poised inches away from my dad's face. I don't know exactly how long the two of them stood there, locked in eye-to-eye combat, but it seemed like an eternity. Eventually, Deacon Myers got the message: Dad wasn't going back down. It was time for the deacon to fish or cut bait. This man decided to fish. To the shock of everyone in the congregation—brother, sister, deacon, Sunday school teacher—Myers reared back and smacked my dad right in the jaw.

This was a defining moment for me.

As a thirteen-year-old, I saw firsthand what it looked like to do the right thing even when it cost something. I sat there and watched my hero, my dad, stand up to the forces of evil and win without firing a shot. I knew then that I wanted to be that kind of man.

But as I was to discover, there is a price to be paid to become a man of character. Integrity and courage are virtues that must be nurtured and developed over time. Desire alone is not enough . . .

After being hit, my dad staggered back for just a moment

and then stepped back up beside Deacon Myers without saying a word. No words were necessary. In an instant my dad, Charles Stanley, had become a hero while Deacon Myers and his cohorts had been exposed as gangsters and thugs. From that moment on, it didn't really matter what anybody said.

Because actions speak louder than words.

7

Struggling with Loss

Though Satan should buffet, though trials should come,
Let this blest assurance control,
That Christ has regarded my helpless estate,
And hath shed His own blood for my soul.
—HORATIO SPAFFORD, 1873

"If we cannot believe God when circumstances seem
to be against us, we do not believe Him at all."
—CHARLES SPURGEON

As I said in the previous chapter, battles are undoubtedly difficult and can wound us profoundly, but the most heartbreaking defeat is what we experience in terms of our loved ones. Nothing in the world can pierce us so deeply or affect us so intensely as the personal losses we endure—when we lose those closest to us to death, discord, or distance. Somehow, those struggles are more impactful, striking at the core of our worth, identity, and security and injuring us down to our innermost parts. No matter what an opponent says or does, it is never quite so damaging as when the wounds come—either intentionally or inadvertently—from someone we love.

That was definitely true for my mother. Until the year she died, she always said with sadness, "You know, the one thing I could never figure out was why God took Charley so early in my life . . . I would have walked through fire for him." Of all she had been through— seeing her mother die, being a single mother, working so hard to support us, experiencing an abusive marriage with my stepfather, and everything else she suffered— losing my father left the greatest chasm in her heart. Certainly, Charley remained the love of her life to the very end.

Nothing in the world can pierce us so deeply or affect us so intensely as the personal losses we endure.

It was a long and difficult road for her. At the end of his life, my stepfather, John Hall, went blind and lost the ability to care for himself. Yet Becca stood by him and took care of him until he died. She once told me that on the day she married him, "I promised God 'for better or worse, until death do us part,' and I'm going to keep my word." She made up her mind that she would never leave him, and she never did.

LOST, BUT FOUND

Mom suffered a stroke shortly after her eighty-third birthday that left her debilitated and needing round-the-clock care. It was hard for her to need so much help when she had been the one to help so many others throughout her life.

On Sunday, November 29, 1992, my mom went home to heaven.

At her funeral, the last thing I wanted to do was to look at her in the casket. I walked around, talked to people, and tried to avoid it however I could. Finally, I got up enough nerve to walk over to the coffin. As I looked in, the Lord reminded me, "Charles, Becca isn't here. She's with Me." Then He brought to mind the awesome truth of 2 Corinthians 5:8, that my mother was "absent from the body and . . . at home with the Lord."

The pastor who preached the message that day had known Becca since she was a teenage girl. He revealed many things about Mom that I never knew before, and I was glad he did. But as I sat under the green tent at the burial site, with Andy on one side and Becky on the other, it struck me that I usually had a different place in the service— at the foot of the casket, with a Bible in my hand, and Scripture to comfort the grieving family. I was usually the one preaching, not the one being consoled. And what shocked me the most was the thoughts of uncertainty that entered my mind. *Suppose there is no resurrection. Suppose I never see Mom again. Suppose this is the very last I will ever be with her.* Those doubts lasted just long enough for me to truly feel their effect. Then all of a sudden, Scripture verse after Scripture verse kept coming to my mind confirming Jesus' promises to us about the resurrection and eternal life:

"I am the resurrection and the life; he who believes in Me will live even if he dies, and everyone who lives and believes in Me will never die" (*John 11:25–26*).

We do not want you to be uninformed, brethren, about those who are asleep, so that you will not grieve as do the rest who have no hope. For if we believe that Jesus died and rose again, even so God will bring with Him those who have fallen asleep in Jesus. For this we say to you by the word of the LORD, that we who are alive and remain until the coming of the LORD, will not precede those who have fallen asleep. For the LORD Himself will descend from heaven with a shout, with the voice of the archangel and with the trumpet of God, and the dead in Christ will rise first. Then we who are alive and remain will be caught up together with them in the clouds to meet the LORD in the air, and so we shall always be with the LORD. Therefore comfort one another with these words (1 Thess. 4:13–18).

"O death, where is your victory? O death, where is your sting?" The sting of death is sin, and the power of sin is the law; but thanks be to God, who gives us the victory through our LORD Jesus Christ (1 Cor. 15:55–57).

That was a powerful moment, one I will never forget. Did I really believe there was a resurrection for those who believe in Christ? Yes! Did I have faith that I would see Mom again? Yes! And did I truly have confidence that we would be together again, that I would dwell with her in the presence of God for eternity? Yes! Yes! Yes!

That was what got me through having to put my mother's body into the ground—the fact that Jesus Christ rose from the grave two thousand years ago. And because He did, we know we will, too (Rom. 6:4; 2 Cor. 4:14).

Did I truly have confidence that we would be together again, that I would dwell with her in the presence of God for eternity? Yes! Yes! Yes!

That is what the apostle Paul meant when he said that we, as believers in eternal life through Christ, do "not grieve as do the rest who have no hope" (1 Thess. 4:13). I had seen how desperate and hopeless grief can be at the first funeral I ever preached. I was at Fruitland at the time, and a man who lived way up in the remote mountains died. Neither he nor his wife believed in Jesus, but his wife asked me to preach the service all the same.

When the service was over, she went to the casket, took hold of his lifeless body, clung to him, and wailed inconsolably. When the ushers tried to pull her away, she began screaming, "You can't leave me! I'll be all alone! I'll have nothing! You can't leave me! You can't leave me!"

It was heartbreaking. She had absolutely no hope—every bit of her security, joy, and confidence lay in that casket, ready to be interred forever.

Thankfully, as believers in Jesus Christ, the grave can't hold our hope. The tomb can't restrain the One who is our everlasting security, joy, and confidence. Because of Jesus, the end here on earth is really only a beginning of a new, better existence with Him. And because of Christ, believers will have a permanent home in heaven, and when we do, absolutely nothing will separate us from our loved ones ever again.

Likewise, through my mother's death, I learned that grief is not something that can or should be cut short. So many people came up to me and said, "Oh, Pastor, we're so sorry about your mother. But isn't it wonderful she's in heaven with the Lord?" Even though I believed it deeply and clung to that hope, it infuriated me when people said it. Why? Because it was like they were trying to short-circuit my grief. But you can't do that. All the pious words in the world will never fill a grieving heart. Rather, you and I must allow the pain to run its full course so that we can experience the healing our heavenly Father intends.

THE PERFECT STORM

Of course, not every loss we experience is due to some external condition. Not every separation is on good terms. Sometimes people choose to walk away. It is an act of volition. And it can hurt even more than losing someone to death.

That is what happened when Annie filed for divorce in 1993. After seeing my mother's example of devotion to John, I was likewise committed to "for better or worse, for richer or poorer, in sickness and in health, until death do us part." So it was especially devastating to have my own wife walk away. After years of my pursuing every possibility of reconciliation I could think of, the divorce was finally granted in 2000.

I loved Anna Margaret Johnson Stanley with all my heart, and regardless of what transpired between us, I never quit loving her to the day she died. Annie passed away on November 10, 2014. She is in the arms of her Savior, and all hurts, all tears, and all wounds have been wiped away. And the truth of the matter is that is how I want people to think of her. I want the world to remember what was best in Annie as the mother of my children and a woman who served God and others with her whole heart. So my prayer is that what lives on from the life of Anna Stanley is all that she did in obedience to Christ. That is what continues on in eternity for each of us.

But as I sit here and reflect on all that was going on at that time, I see that though the Lord was blessing His Word being preached from the pulpit, dark billows of clouds were mounting on the horizon.

As I said in the previous chapter, First Baptist Atlanta was expanding quickly and eventually outgrew its downtown location in the early '90s. On October 16, 1988, the congregation of FBA had voted to buy the Avon property as the new church site, but not everyone wanted to leave the downtown location—and they were very vocal about it.

I understood their concerns. Quite frankly, I didn't like the thought of leaving that historic building either—it had been my home pulpit for more than twenty years. Andy and Becky had grown up there, we'd seen people accept Christ and grow in their faith in that sanctuary, and God had truly done astounding things at that location. So leaving that downtown property was painful for me as well.

My prayer is that what lives on from the life of Anna Stanley is all that she did in obedience to Christ.

It was also very complicated. We had the thirteen downtown properties to sell and the entire Avon building to gut and remodel. Juggling the details of those tasks was overwhelming—especially considering that our space issues at FBA persisted. We still hadn't figured out how to accommodate all the people who were coming to the services.

But I knew it was what God wanted us to do, so I focused on obeying Him. Unfortunately, doing so stirred up a firestorm of dissent in the congregation—a new battle that had many similarities to the others we had faced.

REACHING THE WORLD

That was the first of several pressures that began to take its toll. A second stressor was the great success of In Touch Ministries. When I became the pastor of FBA, the Lord provided us with an opportunity to broadcast *The Chapel Hour* on WXIA-TV 11 and WANX 46.

Eventually, TBS on Channel 17 gave us a time slot as well. Then in 1977, Pat Robertson of the Christian Broadcasting Network called and asked to use some of our sermon tapes. Suddenly the program went from reaching viewers in Atlanta to touching a nationwide audience, but it took quite a bit of effort to adjust our small operation to our new national exposure and exponential increase in correspondence.

At that point, I thought we needed to give the program a more meaningful title that would immediately communicate what it was about. So one day in 1977, while sitting in my study, I looked over to my left, and there on the desk was a *Living Bible* devotional called *In Touch*. I thought to myself, *That's it. That's the goal. I want to get as many people as possible in touch with Jesus Christ and His way of living.* So that is how the name changed from *The Chapel Hour* to *In Touch Ministries*.

As we kept listening to God, He kept opening doors for us— we were adding more television and radio stations constantly. The growth was incredible. But then on one particular morning in August 1989, I was in Kansas City, where In Touch Ministries was holding a rally. I was in my hotel room, on my knees before God, praying to Him about the message I was going to preach later that day. For some reason, Psalm 67:2 kept coming to mind. It says, "Send us around the world with the news of Your saving power and your eternal plan for all mankind" (TLB). I thought, *Well now, what's that about?*

When I was done praying, I got up and looked out the large window at the coliseum where the rally was being held. Right next to it was a rooftop covered with satellite dishes and broadcast antennas. In that moment, God said to me, "That's the way I'm going to do it. That is how I will use you to send the gospel around the world."

I was astounded. Certainly, to be able to minister to people throughout the United States was a great blessing. But to be used by God to reach people worldwide was beyond what this boy from Dry Fork, Virginia, had ever dreamed.

Yet that is what God had in mind. By 1990, the program was airing on Russian television. By 1992, the ministry had established an International Department, a nationwide Prayer Team, and the In Touch Foundation. And by 1994, In Touch's Spanish radio ministry, En Contacto, began airing across North America, Latin America, and other Spanish-speaking countries worldwide. I knew God was well on His way to fulfilling what He had shown me.

A CLASH OF VISION

As you can imagine, the developments at In Touch took a great deal of time and energy. Likewise, the battle at FBA about the move to the Avon building was time-consuming. I was spread thin but focused on serving the Lord obediently and making the most of every opportunity He sent us to broadcast the gospel. And it seemed as if the possibilities for proclaiming God's Word to the nations were unending.

About this time, another issue arose from a wholly unexpected place. For as long as I could remember, whenever anyone asked Andy about his ministry or getting his own church, he would say, "God has given my father an extraordinary platform. I'm here to serve him and help him finish well." I cannot begin to tell you how proud hearing that from my son made me feel. There is nothing that fills a father's heart with such joy as knowing his son is following in his footsteps.

So with that in mind, when we prayed about who would lead our first morning service in the Dunwoody location, the choice was obvious. It had to be Andy. There was no one else I trusted with it. And so on April 19, 1992, he led our first service at the Avon building and began pastoring the new people who began to flock there.

But as you may imagine, the stark dissimilarities in the two buildings resulted in big differences in the worship styles at the two locations. Whereas downtown FBA had all the amenities of a traditional Southern Baptist church—beautiful surroundings, choir and orchestra, and fully equipped facilities—the new campus still resembled a warehouse and had an informal, contemporary atmosphere because of its limited resources. This served to create two separate identities in a church that was supposed to be one congregation.

Likewise, somewhere around this time, Andy traveled with a group of his leaders to South Barrington, Illinois, to Willow Creek Community Church, which was founded by Pastor Bill Hybels, a noted proponent of the contemporary church movement. There, Andy caught Hybels's vision for ways to reach the unchurched. Although Andy and I had the same goal—leading people into a growing relationship with Jesus Christ—the ways we went about it began to diverge in significant ways.

Added to the growing tension between Andy and me was the divorce petition that Annie filed just a year later in 1993. Almost immediately there were calls for me to resign based on the church's policy preventing divorced men from serving as deacons. In addition, pastors and denominational leaders from throughout the country began to join in the outcry for my removal. Not only were friends choosing sides, but my fitness as a pastor became a debate in Christian circles, with longtime opponents and national news outlets rehearsing my every failing.

I prayed and prayed about what to do. And God simply said, "You just keep doing what I called you to do until I tell you differently." So I turned into the storm, just as I always had.

But then came a blow that absolutely devastated me. One day Andy and I were discussing the divorce and the calls for my dismissal. He said, "Dad, you've never asked me what I think you should do."

"Go ahead," I replied. Naturally, I was interested in whatever Andy had to say. But nothing could have prepared me for what he said next.

"I think you should walk into church next Sunday morning and resign. The church needs the opportunity to choose you as its pastor."

Now, after years of going to counseling with him, I understand what he meant. Andy thought that given a vote, the congregation would express its confidence in me as its pastor. He believed that would work strategically to end the debate about whether I should stay or go.

But at the time, it felt very much like betrayal. As I hope you've seen throughout this book, I believe in obeying God and staying the course regardless of the cost. I've never been much for strategies. So at that moment, it sounded to me as if he was siding with my enemies. Instead of encouraging me to stand strong and calling on the forces

God simply said, "You just keep doing what I called you to do until I tell you differently."

against me to stop their onslaught, it appeared that he was advising me to capitulate to them. It also seemed as if he were advising me to succumb to political tactics rather than trusting God.

And the truth of the matter is that I didn't have to call for a vote; my opponents readily did so. In fact, they convened two business meetings. The first was to ascertain whether the congregation wanted me to be pastor if the divorce went through. The vote went over-whelmingly in my favor.

Of course, by then, the rumor mill was churning at full speed. People were continually telling me terrible things about my son, and others constantly bad-mouthed me to him. We were able to overcome it for a while, but eventually such negativity takes its toll on any rela-tionship. There was so much pressure on both of us that on August 3, 1995, Andy came to my office and resigned.

All I could do was walk over to him, put my arms around him, and weep. I felt like I was losing my only son. A few weeks later, he told me he was considering starting a church. I assured him he had my blessing. But all the while, I just kept thinking, *It doesn't have to be this way. He didn't have to leave me to start this church. If he'd just asked me, I would've helped him. Why didn't he trust me enough to share his dreams and confide in me?*

But I suppose that Andy was at the age when young men want to develop their own identities, blaze their own trails, and explore what they are capable of. Had I helped him, he would never have truly known if it were his success or mine. Sadly, Andy's leaving felt to me as if the opportunity to experience God's victories together was gone.

There was also a great deal of fallout from Andy's leaving, and it appeared everything was coming apart at the seams. For example, a second business meeting took place two months after Andy resigned. A group wanted to give the Avon property to Andy outright and make it a brand-new entity. Of course, this would have effectively split First Baptist because of all the congregation had invested in that property. When the majority of the congregation voted that motion down, many people left—some following Andy to his new church.

Likewise, the two-thousand-plus people attending FBA at the Avon building were now without a pastor. So for the next seven months, I preached the 9 a.m. service in Dunwoody and then drove downtown to lead the 11 a.m. service. Finally, on April 6, 1997, First Baptist Atlanta held its last service in the downtown facility. A week later, FBA had all of its services and classes in the north location for the first time—the entire congregation once again residing under one roof.

Well, almost. No one could deny the gaping hole that was left by Andy's departure. But I would not give up my relationship with my son. So I asked Andy to go to counseling with me and invited him to breakfast and lunch as often as I could. And I prayed for him. Constantly.

I am grateful that throughout the years, Andy and I have experienced reconciliation. I love my son dearly—I never for one moment stopped loving him—and I am exceedingly proud of him. From the first time I heard him preach, I knew God would use him in a powerful way—and He has. Andy's North Point Community Church is one

God hasn't called me to understand, but to obey Him, forgive others, and seek forgiveness.

of the largest churches in America and has spread to six campuses throughout Atlanta, reaching untold numbers of people for Jesus. I stand by him no matter what.

I may not comprehend everything that went on during that period of our lives, but I don't have to. Because God hasn't called me to understand, but to obey Him, forgive others, and seek forgiveness.

Jesus says, "Blessed are the peacemakers, for they shall be called sons of God" (Matt. 5:9). Making peace with others takes humility, forgiveness, and trust that God will sort everything out in His time. And that is exactly what we need to live this Christian life.

ADDED TO

Yes, it is always difficult when relationships with the ones we love are broken or lost. But the Father will always support you during those times when you turn to Him. Likewise, He will show you how to move forward. In Psalm 32:8, one of my favorite verses, He says, "I will instruct you and teach you in the way which you should go; I will counsel you with My eye upon you."

For example, along with the encouragement God gave through my daily times of prayer and Bible study, the Father always gave me songs of faith to sustain me. During this particular time in my life, "It Is Well with My Soul" by Horatio Spafford was very meaningful and encouraging:

When peace like a river, attendeth my way,
When sorrows like sea billows roll;
Whatever my lot, Thou hast taught me to know or say
It is well, it is well, with my soul.

I love that song, and the refrain became a theme of my life whenever the Lord would speak peace to the storms I was facing: "It is well with my soul."

God also provided me with dear friends who are still with me to this day. One of them is Tim Olive, the son of missionaries and a professional photographer. We began going on photographic trips during that season.

Each time we arrived at a new location or set up a tripod, we would look for the Father's presence and what He was teaching us through the scenery. After all, as Psalm 34:18 says, "The LORD is near to the brokenhearted and saves those who are crushed in spirit." Certainly, He was actively showing us that we could rely upon Him. It seemed that each day—and sometimes every hour—there were fresh evidences of His love and power on our behalf.

It occurred in both big ways and small. On one trip, I was having a particularly difficult time grieving and dealing with the weight of the loneliness and rejection. We'd been out taking photos along the coast of northern California for a couple of days and hadn't gotten any good shots at all, which only made me feel worse. For some reason I had it on my heart to get a photo of a barn, but in all the locations we went to and all the miles we drove, I never saw even one.

Finally, we were driving along State Route 1 at about eight o'clock at night, so it was dark. We were hungry and tired, so we decided to stop at the next place we found along the way.

When I went to sleep that night, I was low. I was not only mourning the loss of my marriage, but I also wondered how the separation would affect my ministry.

So I prayed, "Father, You know why we're out here. We just want to take photos for Your glory, but we haven't seen anything worth shooting. Lord, You know the heaviness I'm feeling about everything that's happening. I just need to know You still hear me and are in control of everything that concerns me."

Well, the next morning, I got up as usual. I went over to the window, opened the blinds, and just stood there and stared at the incredible sight before me. All the while, I'm thinking, *Hallelujah! Hallelujah! Hallelujah!*

You see, the hotel had given us an ocean-view room, and directly between us and the shore was the most picturesque old barn I'd ever seen—totally surrounded by canna lilies.

I laughed and said, "Tim, get over here. You're not going to believe what you see!"

We couldn't get out there fast enough to photograph those beautiful images. It was absolutely awesome—such a fantastic provision of God's grace. And one of those photographs would eventually be featured on the cover of my book *A Touch of His Peace*. That scene reminded me of what Jesus said in His Sermon on the Mount:

> *"Observe how the lilies of the field grow; they do not toil nor do they spin, yet I say to you that not even Solomon in all his glory clothed himself like one of these. But if God so clothes the grass of the field, which is alive today and tomorrow is thrown into the furnace, will He not much more clothe you? You of little faith! Do not worry then, saying, 'What will we eat?' or 'What will we drink?' or 'What will we wear for clothing?' For the Gentiles eagerly seek all these things; for your heavenly Father knows that you need all these things. But seek first His kingdom and His righteousness, and all these things will be added to you." (Matt. 6:28–33)*

Truly, I had nothing to fear. God would work everything out. Just as He had led us to that barn in the middle of the night when we could barely see where we were going, He would lead me in my life and ministry. No, I could not see the path ahead because of the darkness in my situation, but that didn't matter. He was guiding me and, certainly, He could get me exactly where I needed to go (Ps. 107:29–30). I cannot count how many times God comforted me in such a powerful and meaningful way. It happened again and again—through different circumstances, events, and people.

So many years later, I can honestly say that God has not only healed those wounded places, but He has expanded the scope of the ministry through my losses in ways I could never have imagined. Losing Annie was the worst heartache of my life, but God turned what I thought would certainly destroy the ministry into an opportunity to get the Good News of salvation to a whole new audience of people who would never have listened to me before. In fact, I've had people come up to me since then and say, "For a long time I couldn't watch your program because I thought you couldn't possibly comprehend what I was going through. But now I know you've been there, too, and really understand how I feel." Only God could have engineered that. Only He could have turned the most painful experience of my life into a platform for His glory.

Of course, now that so much time has passed and Annie has gone home to be with the Lord, people often ask me if I would ever consider getting married again. My answer has long been that I personally never felt a freedom to remarry after my divorce. I know there are many different interpretations regarding the Scriptures about divorce and remarriage, and I respect the sincerity of those views. I just knew that it was not God's will for me to remarry.

God has not only healed my wounded places, but He has expanded the scope of the ministry through my losses.

"Aren't you lonely?" I am asked. Yes, sometimes I have some very lonely moments. Like many divorced people, I never dreamed that I would not be married for my entire life. It took a long time for me to accept that I was single again and would probably remain single for the rest of my life. Friday nights used to be the most difficult. I spent many weekend evenings next to a roaring fire, on my knees in prayer, asking God, "Are You sure about this?"

But God, Who never makes a mistake, has been more present with me during my latter years of ministry than ever before. Plus, over the years, He sent me the dearest friends and the most devoted staff a pastor could ask for. I could not be more thankful for or more fulfilled by my fellowship with them and the love they express to me day after day, year after year.

Moreover, God has blessed me with a very special relationship with a woman who prayed for me for many years before I ever knew she was doing so. We became reacquainted long after her husband passed away and I was no longer married. We have enjoyed a wonderful friendship based on praying together and a mutual love of photography. She does not live in Georgia, so much of our communication is by phone. Every Sunday morning she calls to pray with me before I preach. God knew what I needed most during this season of my life—a passionate prayer partner—and He exceeded my heart's desire in Sidney "Sid" Coleman, a woman whom I have grown to deeply love. I am grateful beyond words for our friendship. Neither of us ever wants to do anything to quench the Holy Spirit in our lives. We are both in agreement about our marital status at this time. Sid is God's grace to me personified, and it is *I* who have learned so much about God from her.

YOUR PERSONAL LOSSES

And so my prayer for you is that regardless of your losses, you will stay the course and continue to walk the path that God has called you to walk.

The decision I've made every step of the way is this: "I am going to trust You, God. Wherever You lead, I'll go."

And when you say, "I am going to trust You, Father—no matter what," it changes things. You begin to accept that for whatever reasons beyond your comprehension, the Lord knows what He is doing and that it's the very best for you in some way that is apparent from His eternal viewpoint.

Regardless of the circumstances you encounter on the journey, Christ has encountered them first. And therefore you can say, whether through tears of sorrow or tears of joy, "It is well, it is well, with my soul."

8

Until the Day of Christ Jesus

By faith the church was called to go
In the power of the Spirit to the lost
To deliver captives and to preach good news
In every corner of the earth.
—KEITH & KRISTYN GETTY AND STUART TOWNEND

"Take that which God has given you and share it."
—STEPHEN F. OLFORD

"Jesus Christ is the same yesterday and today and forever" (Heb. 13:8). That fact always fills me with confidence and joyful expectation. In fact, as I write this, I am eighty-three years old, and the future is stretched out before me in a way that is more invigorating and exciting than ever before. I think about Moses, who at eighty had his greatest adventure still before him. Little did he realize that he would spend his latter years being God's man to deliver the people of Israel from their bondage in Egypt, to raise up the next generation of leaders, and to guide them to the Promised Land.

I love that. Because for me, I know that there are still people who have yet to hear the gospel message of Jesus Christ. Likewise, there are promising young men and women to develop into the leaders who will carry on the cause of Christ long after I'm gone. And there are those suffering souls who need to find peace and rest in the Promised Land of Christ's love, grace, and provision. With all this in mind, I am filled with hope.

However, as I watch the news and see the prophecies of Scripture fulfilled one after another, I am struck by how soon Christ's return may actually be. Indeed, the time for Christ's coming is drawing near, and the season for us to proclaim His hope to the nations is growing short.

That is why I often say that anticipating the Lord's return should keep us living productively. Because when we keep our focus on the fact that Jesus could return at any moment, we realize the urgency of getting His message of salvation to all who haven't heard. Of course, "of that day and hour no one knows, not even the angels of heaven, nor the Son, but the Father alone" (Matt. 24:36).

But Jesus did say, "Learn the parable from the fig tree: when its branch has already become tender and puts forth its leaves, you know that summer is near. Even so, you too, when you see these things happening, *recognize that He is near, right at the door*" (Mark 13:28–29; emphasis added).

Later, Christ announced one of the benchmarks: "This gospel of the kingdom shall be preached in the whole world as a testimony to all the nations, and then the end will come" (Matt. 24:14). For almost two thousand years, this seemed impossible because of the enormous scope of the goal and our technological, travel, and transmittal limitations.

But that all began to change in 1895 when Guglielmo Marconi sent the first radio signal, and subsequent advancements were made in the area of communication that would eventually lead to mass broadcasts through the airwaves and even over the Internet. People with a heart for the gospel saw the potential of these innovations to distribute the Good News of salvation to unreached parts. Likewise, the establishment of ministries such as Wycliffe Bible Translators in 1942 made it easier to get the Word of God to the people in their own languages.

Anticipating the Lord's return should keep us living productively.

We are now closer than ever to getting His Word out to all people. With the Bible in more languages and with technological innovations, God has enabled us to reach even the most secluded tribes on the planet. I believe we are living in the most exciting time in history, able to tell so many people in so many different countries about Jesus. Platforms for communication that no one dreamed possible when I was a boy are now everyday tools for taking the gospel around the world.

I am so grateful that God has allowed me to live at such an exciting time in history and that the congregation at First Baptist Church of Atlanta and the staff at In Touch Ministries and I have been able to use these advancements to broadcast the Good News of salvation "to the remotest part of the earth" (Acts 1:8). My sermons have been translated into more than a hundred languages, we are on television and radio stations around the world, and the devices of our Messenger initiative are reaching where normal broadcast channels have not been able to go. In this way, God is using us to make disciples of all the nations and to show them how to follow Christ (Matt. 28:18–20).

ENDING WELL

Have you considered your own role in the spreading of the gospel of Christ? You, too, have gifts to employ for the Kingdom of God, people to reach with the message of salvation, and disciples to raise up to walk in obedience to Christ. And if you believe as I do that at any moment we may see the Lord Jesus face-to-face, then it can and should have an effect on the way you live your life.

So as the Day of our Lord draws near, we should *watch faithfully*. Our lives should be focused on honoring and obeying God so that we can be an authentic testimony to those who don't believe.

We must also *wait peacefully*. As Christians, we don't have to be anxious about the future because no matter what happens, we know Who it is who leads us and watches over us.

We are to *work diligently*, counting on the Holy Spirit to empower us to do whatever the Father asks of us without fear.

And we are to *worship God joyfully*. Each week, we must continue to gather together with other believers to encourage one another, intercede for the lost, and exalt the Lord with a unified voice.

Jesus promises, "Behold, I am coming quickly, and My reward is with Me, to render to every man according to what he has done" (Rev. 22:12).

So consider your life. If Jesus were to return in the next few days or hours, would He find you living for Him? Would He find you watching faithfully, waiting peacefully, working diligently, and worshipping Him joyfully? Would He be able to say that you are fulfilling the purposes for which you were created?

I hope so, my friend, because that is the path to life at its very best.

Yes, it is a road that encounters obstacles, opponents, and

heartbreaks. Sometimes you don't know where you are going or what the next step will be. But you are assured, "Trust in the Lord with all your heart and do not lean on your own understanding. In all your ways acknowledge Him, and He will make your paths straight" (Pr. 3:5–6). You can be absolutely certain that He will always lead you in the right way.

This brings us to the ultimate point of this book, which is my hope that you will join me in this pursuit—serving the Lord, proclaiming the gospel, and fulfilling all you were created for. I pray that through my life's story, you can see all that the Savior can do through the life of an ordinary person who serves an extraordinary God. As the British evangelist Henry Varley said to D. L. Moody, "The world has yet to see what God can do with and for and through and in a man who is fully and wholly consecrated to Him." Because the truth of the matter is, it doesn't matter how you were raised, where you come from, or what challenges you face, you can be the person the Lord works through in unimaginable ways if you'll just obey Him.

Obedience to Christ. That is what I have discovered in these many years I've lived. There is absolutely no life so full of meaning and purpose than the one lived in obedience to Him. Because I know that whatever He calls me to do won't pass away but will continue bearing fruit "until the day of Christ Jesus" (Phil. 1:6).

Like Abraham, I had no idea where following the Lord would take me. But for me, it wasn't where I was going, it was the One who was leading. As Oswald Chambers put it so well, the life of faith and obedience to God includes but is not limited by "intellect or reason, but [it is] a life of knowing Who makes us 'go' . . . a life of tried faith, built on a *real* God." [16]

Endnotes

1. http://www.dol.gov/dol/aboutdol/history/chapter5.htm and http://www.u-s-history .com/pages/h1528.html.
2. W. A. Criswell, "This Grace Wherein We Stand," sermon audio, www.wacriswell.com /Video/MP3s/1954/54–09–12m_TR27.mp3.
3. R. A. Torrey, *The Holy Spirit: Who He Is and What He Does* (Alachua, FL: Bridge-Logos, 2008), p. 50.
4. Ibid., p. 51.
5. Ibid., p. 32.
6. Ibid., p. 41.
7. Ibid., p. 43.
8. Ibid., p. 51.
9. Edward McKendree Bounds, *Preacher and Prayer* (Nashville: M. E. Church Publishing House, 1907), p. 16.
10. V. Raymond Edman, *They Found the Secret: Twenty Transformed Lives That Reveal a Touch of Eternity* (Grand Rapids, MI: Zondervan, 1960), p. 17.
11. Ibid.
12. Ibid., p. 18.
13. Ibid., p. 19.
14. George Müller, *A Narrative of Some of the Lord's Dealings with George Müller* (London: J. Nisbet, 1869–73), p. 470.
15. Ibid., p. 368.
16. Oswald Chambers, *My Utmost for His Highest* (New York: Dodd, Mead, 1935), p. 79.

ALSO BY
CHARLES F. STANLEY

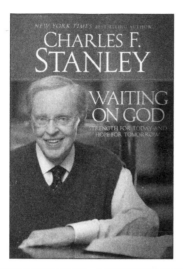

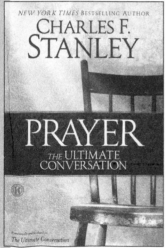

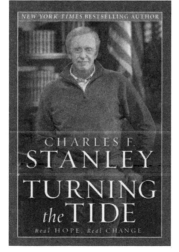

Available wherever books are sold or at SimonandSchuster.com